The Sense of the Supernatural

*He set his eye in their hearts,
to show them the greatness of his works.*
　　　　　　　　　Ecclesiasticus 17:8

THE SENSE OF THE SUPERNATURAL

JEAN BORELLA

Translated by
G. John Champoux

T&T CLARK
EDINBURGH

T&T CLARK LTD
59 GEORGE STREET
EDINBURGH EH2 2LQ
SCOTLAND

Copyright © T&T Clark Ltd, 1998

Authorised English translation of *Le Sens du Surnaturel*.
Copyright © Editions Ad Solem, CH-Genève, 1996.
Tous droits réservés.

All rights reserved. No part of this publication may be reproduced,
stored in a retrieval system, or transmitted, in any form or by any means,
electronic, mechanical, photocopying, recording or otherwise,
without the prior permission of T&T Clark Ltd.

First published 1998

ISBN 0 567 08643 7 (HB)
ISBN 0 567 08662 3 (PB)

British Library Cataloguing-in-Publication Data
A catalogue record for this book is available from the British Library

Typeset by Waverley Typesetters, Galashiels
Printed and bound in Great Britain by Bookcraft Ltd, Avon

Contents

Author's Note — viii
Preface: Nature desires supernature — ix

PART I
THE LOST ROAD OF FAITH: THE BLINDED HEART

1. FROM FAITH-KNOWLEDGE TO FAITH-WILL. — 1
   1. *The advent of ideological Christianity* — 1
   2. *Heresies of the first type are concerned with objective faith* — 6
   3. *Heresies of the second type deal with subjective faith* — 9

2. A VISION DEFICIENT IN LIGHT — 13
   1. *Actual and habitual grace* — 13
   2. *The sense of the supernatural* — 15
   3. *The closing of the eye of the heart and the birth of Modernism* — 17

3. A BRIEF AETIOLOGY OF MODERNISM — 23
   1. *The external causes* — 23
   2. *The internal causes* — 28

4. INVENTORY OF A DEAD FAITH — 31
   1. *From the destruction of nature to a nature shut up within itself* — 31
   2. *Modernism has lost the key to the religious heart of man* — 34

3. Faith has become nothing more than its own historical manifestation	35
4. The Church is only an historical form of religious consciousness	37
5. Divine grace is forgotten	40
6. An established Modernism?	41

5. SPIRIT AND RESISTANCE ... 45
   1. Fidelity to principle, resistance to history ... 45
   2. The resistance of form ... 49
   3. The resistance of spirit ... 53

6. THE SENSE OF THE SACRED ... 59

PART II
THE CONTEMPLATED TRUTH OF FAITH: THE BODY OF CHRIST

7. THE ESSENCE AND FORMS OF THE 'BODY OF CHRIST' ... 69
   1. The triple Body of Christ ... 70
   2. Its unique essence ... 74

8. THE 'BODY OF CHRIST' AND THE WORK OF SALVATION ... 79
   1. The work of creation and the work of salvation ... 79
   2. The mystery of the Blood poured forth ... 84

9. METAPHYSICS OF THE ETERNAL EXPOSITION ... 89

10. THE PROPHETIC AND THE SACRAMENTAL FUNCTIONS OF SCRIPTURE ... 97
    1. Three or four bodies? ... 97
    2. The three co-ordinates of the real and the three phases of Sacred History ... 99
    3. Semantic guidemarks for sacred events ... 101
    4. The sacramental function of Scripture ... 104
    5. Mystery and archetype ... 106

6. Scripture and prayer	107
7. On the metaphysical nature of human and divine-human acts	110
Conclusion: Christ the unity of the Alpha and the Omega	112

Part III
THE REDISCOVERED LIFE OF FAITH: THE DEIFYING GLORY

11. THE SCRIPTURAL AND THEOLOGICAL ROOTS OF DEIFICATION	115
1. Baptismal initiation and divine filiation	115
2. Eucharistic initiation and Christification	119
3. Paracletic initiation and spiritual perfection	120
4. The deifying operations	123
12. FROM DEIFICATION TO CREATION	127
1. Theology or mysticism?	127
2. 'As I will be known, I will know'	130
3. The uncreated Mystery within us	132
4. 'Fiat voluntas tua'	137
Appendix: The Luther Question	143
Index of Names and Subjects	157
Index of Scripture References	160

Author's Note

The first French edition of this book was published in 1981. For the second edition (Geneva: Ad Solem, 1996) the text was revised and expanded by several chapters. The faithful and elegant translation, which G. John Champoux now brings before the English-speaking public, follows the text of this new edition. It has, however, been improved and corrected in a few details. This edition is therefore the definitive one.

JEAN BORELLA

Preface

Nature desires supernature

Some fifty years ago Father de Lubac published *Surnaturel: études historiques*,[1] and one of the major *theological* debates of the twentieth century sprang up around this book. Although almost completely ignored by the public, it occasioned radical confrontations between some of the most illustrious theologians of the Catholic Church. And rightly so, for it touches on what is essential.

The learned Jesuit was not, as the modest subtitle announced, content with retracing the history of an idea, an idea as a matter of fact central to the organisation of Christian doctrine. He also went to work as a theologian to show that ecclesiastical tradition, except for the last two centuries, had never viewed the ideas of a 'pure nature' and a 'pure supernature' as two completely heteronomous realities. In particular he established that the affirmation of a natural desire for the supernatural, which is to say the vision of God, was to be found in St Thomas: 'every intellect naturally desires the divine Substance' (*Summa Contra Gentiles* III, 57). And in fact every being desires its own good for, without it, it cannot attain to its own perfection; thus the intellect, whose proper good is the Truth of that which is, necessarily aspires to the knowledge of That which absolutely is: 'consequently, for perfect happiness the intellect needs to reach the very Essence of the First Cause. And thus it will have its perfection through union with God as with that object' (*Summa Theologiae* IaIIae, 3, 8).

---

[1] Paris: Aubier, 1946. See also Henri de Lubac, *The Mystery of the Supernatural* (New York: Crossroad, 1998), originally published in France in 1965.

The Sense of the Supernatural

Now, if God has created the intellect in such a way that it can realise the perfection of its nature only by gaining access to the knowledge of Perfect Being, then since God does nothing in vain, it follows that union with God is owed to the intellect by virtue of its very nature; 'if the intellect of the rational creature could not reach so far as to the first cause of things, the natural desire would remain void' (*Summa Theologiae* Ia, 12, 1).

For man, then, there is no natural finality; his nature is only completed by supernature. Man's destiny is naturally supernatural. But then, if we admit these conclusions, do we not risk destroying the gratuitousness of grace and subjecting it to the necessity of nature? This is what the encyclical *Humani generis* (1950) explicitly meant to condemn: 'Others [Lubac is being targeted here] destroy the gratuity of the supernatural order, since God, they say, cannot create intellectual beings without ordering them and calling them to the beatific vision' (IIa, 4). This semi-condemnation, in which he saw above all a misunderstanding of his own theses, was strongly resented by the future cardinal. He yielded, however, as an obedient son of the Church, and withdrew from teaching theology.

In this 'affair' – and the greater public heard only a faint echo of it – the very meaning of Christianity was at stake, as the crisis inaugurated by the Council would reveal. Also, if the thinking of Father de Lubac had been better understood, we would have avoided a few conflicts and much devastation, which brought the collapse of entire sectors of the most traditional and most basic theology. In my opinion, matters have proceeded as they did at the beginning of the nineteenth century with the condemnation of traditionalism and ontologism: justified with precise terminology, these condemnations nevertheless disqualified two movements of thought which, alone, had taken the true measure of what Kantian rationalism and revolutionary ideology implied. The result was the explosion of Modernism at century's end for want of doctrines able to offer a truly profound response to the questions posed by the evolving sciences and philosophies. Likewise, the critics of the future cardinal were right to adopt a strict definition of terms. For if we speak of the nature of a being, we speak of what it is as such and without which it would not partake of being. If the vision of the Divine Essence is a natural requirement for the human being, just as air is a natural requirement for mammals, God can no more create intelligent life without bestowing himself on it than he can create an animal with pulmonary respiration without creating air to breathe. 'God and nature', says Aristotle, 'do nothing in vain.'

I will not enter into a debate which exceeds my competence and which only indirectly concerns the object of my book. However, it seems that the fear of seeing the thesis of a natural desire for the supernatural destroying the gratuity of grace is the result of an overemphasis on the Aristotelian idea of the natural order. There is, in Aristotle, a tendency to naturalism, to consider the aggregate of beings as a rigid system of natures complete in themselves, beings perfectly formed and fully consistent in their order, and to think that such grounds are sufficient to drain them of mystery. Nature *of itself*, in such a view, excludes the supernatural, just as, of itself, the circle excludes the square.

This naturalism is not it seems altogether Christian, nor truly in conformity with what is taught in Revelation as presented by either the Old or New Testament. Perhaps it does not even conform to what Aristotle taught, with whom, it is said, a certain 'supernaturalism' of the intelligible form saw the light of day. However this may be, it seems hard to admit that the natural order is complete and autonomous of itself, whether this involves man or creation in general. Quite the contrary: we believe that, in and by themselves, both man and the world are incomplete. There is no state of 'pure nature', save in God at the level of the Eternal Ideas, for which the Word is the prototypical synthesis. Even in Paradise the Garden had to be kept and *cultivated*, and all of the beings of nature laboured to realise themselves. This is the cosmic work in which each thing is striving to rejoin its essence, but, by definition, without ever attaining it altogether; otherwise it would truly mean the end of becoming. After all, does not St Paul say that 'all creation groaneth and travaileth in pain, even till now' (Rom. 8:22)? Along with us, it is hoping for its glorification and renewal. But this does not mean that God might be constrained in some way to satisfy this expectation, and that divine freedom might be subject in this way to the order of the world. This order is, in fact, never so consistent, nor so rigorously linked to what we grasp of causal relationships (such and such a principle, such and such a consequence), that every disorder would be equivalent to the negation of the One who is its Author. The ways of divine Wisdom are truly impenetrable.

The Sense of the Supernatural

The sense of the supernatural is first the awareness of a radical lack in the very substance of the natural human order, the awareness of a relative incompleteness, and of a dissatisfaction with respect to the nobility of our spirit: not the pride of an intelligence which would find within itself the promise and the guarantee of its 'divine' destiny, but, to the contrary, the recognition that nothing of the natural, not even the reasonable animal that we are, is truly worthy of this transnatural miracle that is our spirit. To have the sense of the supernatural is to understand that 'man infinitely surpasses man', and that there is nothing in nature which corresponds to the spirit: 'Thou hast made us for thyself, Lord, and our heart is restless till it rest in thee.'

But to have the sense of the supernatural is also to know that God always gives more than he promises. Thus the satisfaction of the natural desire to see God is not this desire's projection into mere emptiness, in such a way that God by satisfying it would only have to make a few adjustments. This idea, perhaps 'Aristotelian', is altogether insufficient and lets what is essential escape. When God fulfils a desire, he fulfils it *beyond all measure*, and therefore nothing can measure this fulfilment beforehand. This is why, in reality, we do not know what we desire, even and above all when we desire to see God. And this is why every fulfilment is grace, and grace already our desire for it, grace which hollows out in us the place for God.

In writing this book, my specific intent was to reopen within ourselves this very place where God awaits our waiting on him. The modern world has been built up out of a complete naturalisation of human and cosmic nature. The dominant scientifico-philosophical thinking has only broken from Aristotle by going to the extreme of his naturalist tendency, that is to say by rejecting the supernaturalism of the intelligible forms, and therefore by closing nature in upon itself, by rendering it impermeable to grace by ontological self-sufficiency. It is with this world closed upon its own physical and purely material reality that the proposal of the Church's faith has clashed. But whether the most official theology has been aware of this is uncertain, despite the philosophical warnings of a Maurice Blondel. Convinced that scholastic philosophy was the expression of natural reason, of a reason independent of all revelation and utilising its own laws, it thought itself still able to speak in this language to a society which had only the words 'nature' and 'reason' on its lips. In agreeing

PREFACE

with European science to treat natural things rationally according to natural reason, it hoped that it might admit further that to envision a 'supplement of soul' was not unreasonable: admit the proposal of a revealed message, in essence supernatural, which, as a consequence, would not compete with the domain of science. What an illusion! There were no shared meanings for the concepts of nature and reason. And soon the human sciences would show that Aristotle's philosophy, far from being an expression of reason in the natural state (why it and not any other non-revealed doctrine?), was one cultural product among others. All of the modernisms have sprung from this.

Sadly, history thus seems to have decided the debate occasioned by Father de Lubac's book in his favour, to have proved him right. By developing a completely non-sacral line of thought, a line of thought totally foreign to anything which might refer to the supernatural, modern culture has proved, *a contrario*, that the reception of the grace of faith is impossible without an opening in our nature through which this grace can penetrate and quicken us; an opening which is none other than the 'spiracle of life' (the 'airhole')[2] that the God of Genesis breathed into the face of Adam. And, because our nature includes the intellect, and because it is also (and even first of all) to the intellect that the proposal of faith is addressed, we must indeed suppose an innate capacity, as minimal as it may be, for finding meaning in what is supernatural.

It is time to stop proposing faith solely to our moral and humanitarian sense, to our natural affective powers, and finally awaken this sense of God that, by creating us, God has lodged in our hearts.

Nancy
24 July 1996

---

[2] *Translator's note*: When God breathes into the face of Adam, this act both creates an aperture and imparts the breath of life at the same time. Cf. the author's *La charité profanée* (Bouère: Editions Dominique Martin Morin, 1979), pp. 179–80, and *The Secret of the Christian Way: A Contemplative Ascent through the Writings of Jean Borella*, ed. and trans. G. John Champoux (Albany, NY: SUNY Press, forthcoming), chap. 6.

Part I

THE LOST ROAD OF FAITH:
THE BLINDED HEART

Chapter 1

From Faith-Knowledge to Faith-Will

1. *The advent of ideological Christianity*

For ideological Christianity, Christian identity is defined as the minimal aggregate of beliefs necessary for the moral support of those undertakings imposed by the universal fraternal struggle. In general we may say that the task of every ideology is to establish theoretically and, even more, to justify emotionally some social, political, economic, aesthetic, ethical practice or other: to supply these practices with the ideo-psychological nourishment needed for their existence and pursuit. Ideologies, it has been said, are the true mythologies of the modern world. They are not all situated on the same level – some are more foundational or more nurturing than others – but every domain of activity can be 'ideologised': science, history, man, the body, sex, commerce, freedom, happiness and (obviously) God. In the twentieth century, the ideologies of race and of the nation state, or those of the 'sense of history' and of the dictatorship of the proletariat, have been used to justify the most monstrous crimes the world may have ever known. Today, feminist ideology, linked to that of freedom, is supposed to justify the physical elimination of any human embryo perceived as inconvenient. There is ideology, then, each time a theoretical utterance assumes the form of a principle, all the while drawing its authority not from on high and from pure Truth, as it should, but from below and simply from the need to justify a particular practice. Ideology is thus the occasion for a reversal of the normal relationship between theory and practice. The value of principles is, in fact, necessarily inherent to their intrinsic truth: they are free because transcendent, escaping every contingency and variation of time and place; hence their axiological power. Otherwise, changing at the need of whims and circumstances, they would have only the appearance of transcendence, and their power to justify would be simply that of our desires and passions nobly disguised.

The order of religion should be, pre-eminently, the order of transcendent truths; 'pre-eminently' since here it is the Transcendent itself, the Principle as such, which descends toward men and reveals the loftiest of truths. No merely speculative declaration possesses an equal authority. If, then, we distinguish in faith a *material* object (which is the matter of faith, what we believe, the content of faith) and a *formal* object (the fact that such a statement is formally considered to be 'of the faith'), we understand that what establishes such and such a truth *as* a truth of faith, and the motive by which we adhere by faith to such a declaration, is the 'authority of a revealing God' (First Vatican Council): such and such a declaration is 'of the faith' *because* God has revealed it. The Church has, then, no other authority than that which its fidelity to the revealed deposit confers, having the right to propose its doctrine only by reason of its divine origin. This origin alone is able to adorn the articles of the Catholic *Credo* with the form of 'transcendent truth' which is theirs, thanks to which they are preserved from all risk of subjection to the interests or passions of the moment. Though present, by their very content, in human history and therefore to some extent compromised by it (the Church being somewhat at the mercy of time), there is within them an originating principle by which they escape every 'instrumentalisation' and conjunctive refashioning.

Without doubt the principles of the sciences, and metaphysical science most particularly, enjoy an equal independence. But metaphysical principles are known and certified by themselves: the human mind sees their transcendent truth as a need immanent to its own intellectual activity. It is not the same for the truths of faith: no intellect discovers them within itself; it receives them from elsewhere. Hence the need for an unconditional authority.

Leaving aside, then, the case of metaphysical principles, we can see that only a 'theological form' is able to safeguard the declarations of the Christian faith from being invested by an ideological form. To renounce the former, or simply to lose sight of it, is to make it vulnerable to the latter – to 'cast pearls before swine', to hand over God's Truth to the vicissitudes of human

From Faith-Knowledge to Faith-Will

egoism, completely depriving it of all saving and liberating power.

And yet, for thirty years, a kind of mutation has been occurring in the faith of Catholicism: not only are we seeing, as we have always seen, laity and former priests reject all or part of Christian dogma, but we are also encountering with some frequency priests (and even bishops), theologians, and exegetes who, all the while wishing to be of the Church, place in doubt many of the truths which the Church has always held and continues to hold as truths of faith guaranteed by divine authority. This is a 'sociologically' new phenomenon. The Church has known many heresies and heretics: in general they have left the Church or abandoned their error. Today it is no longer the same. But are these 'mutant' Christians heretics? A heretic is one who has made a choice (*hairesis* = choice) from among the truths to be believed. These new Christians do not choose: in a certain way they accept all or nearly all of the traditional faith, but only by giving it a different meaning. Here hermeneutics has devoured its object; hence the multiplicity of interpretations, no longer seeing in this faith any objective reality which might provide a basis for and orient one towards an understanding of it. Such Christians are not exactly 'heretics', since they publicly lay claim to the title of Catholic and affirm their membership in the Church. Often, they will go so far as to denounce the insupportable dictatorship of the Roman magisterium whenever it formulates the least call to orthodoxy.[1] All of this is quite paradoxical: either the adjective 'Catholic' has a definite meaning, a *real* identity made exact in a body of recognised truths, or else it designates a purely nominal belonging, a simply *formal* identity, a label: in which case it is hard to see what interest one may have in wanting to be a Catholic, unless for some social benefit still to be derived.

What is surprising and almost inconceivable is not that Catholics, whether priests or laity, experience great difficulties in admitting the virginity of Mary, the divine origin of Jesus, his miracles, original sin, the redemption of the human race at the price of Christ's blood, the Resurrection and Ascension, the

---

[1] This is so for Hans Küng and Eugen Drewermann, to cite only the most famous cases.

identity of the sacrifice of the Mass and the sacrifice of the Cross, eucharistic transubstantiation, the life of the soul separated from the body, the perpetuity of hell, the Assumption of Mary, etc.; this is not surprising because, in reality, these truths are hardly believable and have *always been so*. In the past, one gave one's faith to them, one held them to be certain because the Church attested that it held them from God. Nothing could be more difficult, but also nothing more simple: faith reposing on the argument of the divine authority of Christ. At least it was perfectly *logical*: we either believe this or not. And we believe in the faith of the Word of God transmitted by the Church, because *of and by ourselves* we obviously have no means of knowing if such things exist, or of being assured that such things are true. From this point of view Christians of every age have rallied to the same standard, while history shows that modern unbelief has invented nothing new.

The true novelty is that so many authorised clerics, so many experts in exegesis and theology, and at times so many bishops,[2] under the pretext that these truths, these dogmas, these sacred facts escape our ordinary experience of the real or our usual ways of conceptualising, have quite simply ceased to believe in them, seeing just images, cultural representations elaborated by the primitive community according to the 'mythifying' needs of its religious imagination. This is something unheard of: a Church (not in its supreme magisterium, or in the simple faithful, but in the actual practice of the faith of a part of its clergy and intellectuals) that ceases to hold as true and real what it did for two thousand years! And this accompanied by a general silence and a kind of indifferent acquiescence from Catholic society, when such an infidelity should howl in our ears. How do we explain the strange torpor into which the Christian conscience has plunged? Is it not because these new theologians find themselves in deep and solid agreement with *the faith of our times*, with the Christian soul of the twentieth century? They claim, these Fathers of the New Church, that they want to express the Catholic faith in a language accessible to today's people. What an imposture! Having put the

---

[2] One episcopal collection of catechetical documents has presented the Ascension of Christ as a simple 'manner of speaking'.

teaching of the Church in parentheses – such is the rule of the exegetes – far from starting their explanations with the immutable contents of traditional faith in their explanations (as simple logic would require), they in fact start with the ideology of the modern world posed as an *a priori* and as the sole criterion of faith. *De fidei* is that which suits the needs of our times; our new fidelity is to these needs alone. What Christian ears are made to hear is not the hard truth of the eternal Word, but the servile and complaisant echo of the fleeting convictions and infatuations of the moment: a 'sociologically correct' faith.

What has happened to produce such a mutation? What was needed for the formal object of faith to disappear, for the authority of the revealing God to cease being its argument and foundation, for what was difficult but normal not so long ago suddenly to cease having any weight? Surely, since authority is involved, one must say that the authority of God has been replaced by another: the authority of public opinion among the pastors and, among the theologians, that of an ideologised science (either physical or social) whose conclusions have been poorly understood or even misunderstood. This is incontestable.[3] But how has such a substitution become possible? How did so many Christians come to forget, not the content of the truths themselves (since they still make a case for them, albeit only to demythologise), but the faith that these truths demand? For this clearly involves faith, and it is therefore the mystery of faith that we are called upon to investigate: it alone, if anything, will account for this mystery of iniquity that has been at work beneath our very eyes. The Christian soul has lived by these truths, not as one kind of nourishment that might eventually be replaced by another, but as the only food suited to its Christian nature, since in fact *God made it to be so*. How is it possible that, within a few years, we have come to lack even the least memory of this primary rule, and are trying to keep our Christian soul alive with 'truths' unsuited to its diet? Why do these eternal truths, handed on to us by the perennial tradition of the Church, no longer have the savour of Life for us?

[3] I have shown this in *La crise du symbolisme religieux* (Lausanne: L'Age d'Homme, 1990).

But where does this enquiry lead? It leads to a level of analysis of the faith more profound and more hidden than that of its formal object. As we have seen, the advent of ideological Christianity (or, if you prefer, Christo-humanism) can be described as a disappearance of the very form of faith, an obliteration of the idea of divine authority, an idea which has purely and simply vanished from religious consciousness.[4] But the formal object of faith makes sense only in terms of its material object. If faith requires the guarantee of divine authority, this is so that its matter may be received into our soul: the essential thing is still its content. Therefore in this content, in the truths to be believed, there has to be something so foreign to our way of thinking that the very weight of divine authority (coupled with the fear of eternal damnation) is no longer enough to make us accept it. We need to confront at last this dreadful situation of modern man and try to understand it.

2. *Heresies of the first type are concerned with objective faith*

I shall begin with a somewhat unusual consideration, but one which will appear to be quite obvious on reflection. The history of heresy in the Church has been more than just a series of occasions for defining the essential dogmas of our faith. Unquestionably, the negation of any given doctrinal point has ultimately been of benefit in that it has led to the clear definition of that point, and 'there needs must be heresies'. But not enough has been made of the fact that these heresies also reveal some pertinent elements involved in an act of faith. Just as a physical illness can make us aware of a particular organ, so also the history of doctrinal illness can shed light on certain elements in the act of faith of which we would otherwise be quite unaware.

In point of fact, it is not so much the specific heresies that provide this revelatory function as it is their form or type. This is the reason why the relationship of heresiology to these structural elements is not immediately apparent. Also, to the extent that the early heresies were of a single type, only a single element in the act of faith was brought to light. Because of this

---

[4] As a stunned public opinion proves when the Pope enlists his infallibility to reject the ordination of women.

there was a tendency to see in faith only this element – to reduce faith to this element alone. This does not mean that there is a history or an evolution of faith. But there is a history of the various ways in which we have looked at faith, a history which, in its various phases, successively reveals the constituent elements in the act of faith.

Until the fifteenth century the multiple heresies arising from the bosom of Christianity were all essentially of a doctrinal character. As stated above, heresy consists in *choosing* from the totality of the dogmatic corpus (the teachings of the Church) those truths which one accepts and those which one either rejects or alters. It is essential to understand the nature of this dogmatic corpus. If the primary reason for faith is the authority of God revealing what should be believed, and what could not be grasped by our reason acting alone, then it follows that the effect of this unique and divine origin is the formation of an ensemble of truths which are organically linked to one another, a unified body of teachings whose *intrinsic coherence* is constantly verified. Theological effort, the exercise of reason, could not by itself demonstrate any of these truths received from revelation, but this effort can show their internal and mutual coherence. This very coherence is the basis for the solidity of the dogmatic corpus, and has allowed Catholic doctrine to triumph over every attempt to reduce or fragment it in the first part of its history. Rather than demonstrate the falsity proper to each heretical proposition, the Church has conquered by demonstrating its incompatibility with the rest of her teachings. The dogmatic corpus has prevailed by the strength of homogeneity.

Now what is remarkable is that, despite their diversity, these heresies implicitly agreed upon one point. Faith was seen by one and all as the adherence of the intelligence to truths whose content alone mattered. The adherence, the subjective act which leads human beings to give their assent, was in some manner absorbed by the content, the object of faith adhered to. It was over the object of faith that they argued, and it was this that constituted faith, be it Catholic or non-Catholic. Such a concept of faith-truth is situated from the very beginning on the intellectual level, a level which has been obviously beyond the reach of our contemporaries for quite some time. Hence it follows that they are not about to believe in what they have forgotten, namely that faith was first of all a commitment to the Word of Jesus Christ and the love of neighbour. It was for this that the theologians testified with their blood, not hesitating to give up their lives for Christ and their brothers. The highly intellectual Origen dedicated his whole life to preaching such truths, and died of the consequences, undergoing martyrdom at an advanced age. So also St Justin, St Maximus the Confessor and innumerable others. But this was because attachment to Jesus Christ (and to neighbour for the love of Jesus Christ) was a self-evident truth. And all the heresies of the time were above all *Christian* heresies, arising out of a Christian framework. Even the heresies of Sabellius, Arius and Nestorius involve a degree of theological faith incomparably greater than anything we see today. These divergences arose in connection with knowing just who this Jesus Christ was; but with regard to such issues as the nature of religion, belief in the supernatural, the greater importance of the divine and heavenly relative to the human and earthly, there was unanimity. The pagans themselves were deeply religious people: for them there was no doubt about the existence of an invisible and all-powerful world.

Thus, heresies of the first type reveal an essentially objective conception of faith in which the intellect, the pre-eminent faculty of objectivity, plays a central although not very visible role – not very visible both because of the intellect's transparency and because of its innate capacity to let us receive within ourselves something other than ourselves. This is why the Council of Trent affirms, against the Lutherans, that, by virtue of its objective nature, faith would not be lost by a lack of charity, that is to say by a lack in commitment to the truths one believes. In this 'theological' period we have been discussing, we see the faithful go straight to the essential; what is most important for them is to know whether something is *objectively* true or false, *objectively* real or illusory, because what matters is what *is*, and not the more or less lively feeling of commitment experienced by our consciousness.

And yet the Reformation movement inaugurated by Luther leads us toward just such a conception of faith: the substitution of subjective faith for objective faith, of fiducial faith (faith-confidence) for doctrinal faith, of faith-sentiment for faith-knowledge; a substitution which could only entail a complete

From Faith-Knowledge to Faith-Will

relativisation of the dogmatic corpus and its power of internal coherence. And this is why we should briefly analyse this second heresiological type, which calls into question a subjectively more profound element of the act of faith – the will.

3. Heresies of the second type deal with subjective faith[5]

'Theology', Dr Martin Luther declares, 'is chiefly custom and practice, and does not consist in speculation or in reflecting on the things of God by the use of reason.'[6] The chief care of the Reformer, a concern for the moral order, shows through this assertion; Protestantism is first a moral revolt against what appears to be unworthy of God. Its original impulse was not occasioned by a disagreement in the doctrinal order, but by a burning anxiety for the honour of God – which is indeed the subtlest of snares by which the Devil baits our pride. What was insupportable was not so much that some dogmatic thesis was deemed false in itself, but that it should be attributed to God or thought to be a concern of his. In his eyes, the rejected dogmas were not so much *errors* as *blasphemies* and sacrilege. Obviously, with such an attitude, the Reformer has set himself up as guardian and protector of God's honour. But the pride which this implies is as it were justified by the nobility of the task which he has arrogated to himself. Only in this way can we grasp the inseparability of the two aspects – one individual and the other communitarian – of the Lutheran reform.

As we know, the theory of justification by faith alone came to the young Luther as a liberating intuition, an intuition that put an end to the terrifying agony which had afflicted him with a feeling of damnation. This insurmountable agony already testifies to a considerable weakening of the speculative function: doctrinal truths, as conceived of in his understanding, were powerless to allay his distress of soul. Intellectual certitude being ineffective and basically non-existent, he craved an existential and subjective certitude. Now, with respect to God, there is no other existential certitude, humanly speaking,[7] than that of a

---

[5] See the appendix on the Lutheran question at the end of the book.

[6] Cf. *Propos de table* (Paris: Editions Aujourd'hui), p. 240.

[7] This reservation is imperative because, in the supernatural order, there is also divine grace; but, in its source, it is of God.

living and experiential faith. Even though Luther lacked certitude with regard to the dogmas of the Church, he could not doubt his own will to believe.

But can this subjective faith, reduced to the sentiment of one's own will to believe, constitute a sure sign of salvation capable of tearing out of us the agonising fear of damnation? After much study, Luther thought he had found an affirmative answer in St Paul, who says in the epistle to the Romans that 'the just live by faith'. Faith is thus the life of the just. And who are the just? Not those who are judged to be such, but those who are *rendered* such, who have been established in a state of justice; this is what is called justification. And what is faith? It is believing in Jesus Christ, who has ransomed us by his death. Now it is precisely this faith which, according to St Paul, will be *imputed as justice*. Hence, to be justified (= sanctified), nothing more than belief in being saved by Christ is required of us, which is to say, nothing more than *belief in the certitude of salvation*. To doubt this is to rank oneself among the reprobate; to believe that Jesus Christ saves us is to be saved, since it is this faith alone which God requires of us.

This discovery, which is more of a mental set than an intuition, not only had the effect of appeasing Luther's agony and 'opening [to him] the gates of Paradise',[8] it also entailed a certain idea of justice and of the only kind of faith worthy of God. Here once again we find that concern for God's honour, which I consider to be the mainspring of Protestantism's psychological dynamism.

As for justification, it does honour to God because it attributes to the justice of Christ alone the justification of the sinner, a justification by which 'he covers us':[9] this is external or forensic justice. 'This justification of God [passive justification] *by which he is justified by us* is our justification by God.'[10] We ourselves are in fact completely incapable of any good. Our nature is sinful and remains *so even in justification*, for this justification belongs

---

[8] Cf. the preface written by Luther for the 1545 general edition of his works, trans. L. Cristiani, *Luther tel qu'il fut* (Paris: Fayard, 1955), p. 61.
[9] Cf. ibid., p. 63.
[10] Cf. Schol. 3, 4, Weimar edn. (hereafter *WA*), vol. 56, p. 226; cited by Charles Boyer in *Luther, sa doctrine* (Rome: Presses de l'Université grégorienne, Rome, 1970), p. 41.

uniquely to Jesus Christ. The goodness of human nature being entirely destroyed, no work is good in and of itself: 'every work of the just is damnable and a mortal sin, if God so judges it'.[11] This is why 'the saints, even though they are just, are sinners at the same time. They are just only because they believe in Jesus Christ who *covers* them . . .; sinners because they do not fulfil the law.'[12]

As for faith, it does honour to God because it consists uniquely in bestowing its confidence upon his evangelic word: 'Our faith accords to God the honour of being able to do and of wanting to do what he promised, namely to justify sinners.'[13] In other words, if we wish to render justice to the text of Scripture, to render due honour to his word, we must adopt the Lutheran exegesis and reject papism along with its concept of a justice 'inherent' to the nature of a human being; we must reject the doctrine of grace, whose proper work for Catholics is not to suppress nature, but to perfect it.[14]

This is why, for the believing Lutheran, the moral imperative to honour God also obliges him to reject the Catholic Church, whose very structure (not merely its sins) is an offence to God. And so it is no surprise that the Lutheran revolt essentially manifests itself in a hatred of the Roman institution, and in the formation of a Church which wants to be a pure spiritual community of believers. This further explains why Protestantism, by virtue of its ethical and moral nature, sees orthodoxy only from the viewpoint of orthopraxy or right practice. Effective Christian practice is for it the sign of true faith and doctrine. And so, it is clear to see, by reducing the act of faith to the element of will we are forced to reduce theology to morality

---

[11] Text cited by Boyer, *Luther, sa doctrine*, p. 40 (WA, vol. 7, pp. 138, 29–30 and vol. 56, pp. 347, 9–14.

[12] Ibid.

[13] *Propos de table*, vol. 1, p. 191.

[14] 'The papists are drowned in their idea of "inherent justice"', *Propos de table*, vol. 1, p. 189. For Catholic theology, justice (or holiness), which is a grace, is not in itself a reality (a substance); it has need then of a substantial reality, the very being of the just, to which it is inherent (or adherent). This doctrine, which satisfies the demands of both reason and faith, signifies that God's love is addressed to our very being, not to annihilate it or render it useless in its own sanctification, but to transform and divinise it.

and orthodoxy to orthopraxis. Right faith expends itself in just conduct. Now the Church as an historically and socially defined reality expresses the ensemble of rules which determine Christian life and behaviour. It is, as it were, the objective and visible synthesis of an effectively practised faith. There is no room in Christian action, then, for two authentic Churches, for two authentic practices of Christianity: one excludes the other, because every act, at the moment of its accomplishment, excludes every other act. The Greek schism has truly cut off Rome from a part of herself, and we hope for an eventual reconciliation under the authority of the Vicar of Christ. But the making of a new Church out of Protestantism has taken nothing away from the Roman Church; it has purely and simply 'suppressed' and 'replaced' her. Ecumenism is meaningless here; it is not *reunification* but *conversion* that matters. Protestantism is not a portion of the unique Christian Church; to itself it is the only 'true Christianity'. And, whether we like it or not (I am speaking without the least passion), if Protestantism does not become Catholic, Catholicism will become Protestant.[15]

Such then is the second type of heresy presented to us by history. In the act of faith, it chiefly discloses the element of will. It is essentially concerned with the Christian way of acting and, because of the exclusive nature of every practice when set up as an orthopraxy, it is necessarily expressed in the formation of a new Church; whereas the first type of heresy was essentially concerned with the Christian way of knowing and is necessarily expressed in the definition of dogmatic theses.

---

[15] This mutual incompatibility of two forms of the Christian way of acting does not exclude certain complementarities: a Catholic can find positive aspects in Protestantism, aspects which the Roman Church has not always known how to develop. This is incontestable; and Luther has even said very beautiful things about the Church. In the order of historical considerations, perfect types are not to be found. But these complementarities are secondary.

Chapter 2

A Vision Deficient in Light

Christian *being*, the only element in the act of faith not yet placed in doubt, is the object of the third type of heresy. Although man is both intellect and will, he is even more profoundly a being, an ontological subject, a real person. If the act of faith demands the adherence of the intelligence and the movement of the free will, it also requires, beyond and previous to this, a receptivity to the supernatural grace of faith on behalf of the individual – the spiritual or personal being – who is the common root of intellect and will.

That this receptive capacity is as concerned with the intellect as it is with the will – and that it is therefore a disposition of their common principle – is clearly apparent once we notice, like St Thomas, that the will itself can move the intellect only on condition that it possess a kind of pre-existent knowledge of that *towards which* it moves the intellect.[1] No matter how the question is examined it is always possible to discover a trace of the will in intellection and a trace of the intellect in volition. This presupposes a common centre for these two aspects or powers, and this is the personal being.

1. Actual and habitual grace

We turn now to a consideration of grace, not because of its already established relationship with the will and intellect, but rather because, without this divine assistance, no one can raise the natural powers of the soul to the supernatural level of a true and constant adherence to faith. This grace assists the intellect in the *act* by which it grasps revealed truths, and assists

---

[1] *Summa Theologiae* IIaIIae, 8, 4.

the will in the *act* by which it desires that to which the intellect applies itself. This is why the term 'actual grace' is given to this divine help. It is the momentary help which accompanies the intellect and will each time they truly accomplish an act of faith. This actual grace can attain an exceptional degree, as when, for example, St Thomas luminously delves into the understanding of a dogma, or when the will of a martyr maintains an unshakeable constancy in the faith.

Actual grace is, however, subordinate to another grace which is concerned, not with the powers of the soul, but with the onto-logical subject of these powers, the personal being. This grace is called 'habitual' because of the permanent character it stamps upon the essence of the soul. A *habitus* in fact designates an inclination or permanent capacity: as, for example, a mathematician possesses the *habitus* for mathematics, even when he is not actually doing mathematics, and in this differs from someone ignorant of the subject. A *habitus* generally predisposes one to accomplish a work and is thus called an *operative habitus*. (In his *being* a mathematician is no different from a non-mathematician.) Now the *habitus* conferred on us by the primary grace of faith is not at first concerned with the Christian way of acting; this *habitus* is infused directly into our very being and is called an *entitative habitus* because it is concerned with an entity: the essence of the soul, the immortal person. What this means is that habitual grace effects a real change in our soul, a change by which our very being is opened up to the awareness of supernatural realities.

The great majority of theologians hold that faith, in its beginnings, in its initial principle, is a supernatural work springing from a prevenient sanctifying grace 'supernatural in its very substance'.[2] And this is basically what the Council of Trent affirmed in stating that 'in justification [= in sanctifying grace], man receives [through Jesus Christ], simultaneously with the remission of sins [= baptism], all the infused gifts: faith, hope and charity.'[3] And St Thomas, who carefully distinguishes the infused virtues (like faith) from sanctifying grace, writes: 'grace, being something anterior to virtue, should likewise have

[2] Abbé Berthier, *Abrégé de théologie dogmatique et morale*, 4ème édition (Lyon-Paris: Librairie Catholique Emmanuel Vitte, 1927), n. 745.
[3] Sixth session, chap. 7.

for a subject something anterior to the powers of the soul, namely *its very essence* . . . Just as the soul's essence emanates its powers, which are, in their turn, the various principles of its works, so the virtues emanate from grace into the powers of the soul.'[4]

2. *The sense of the supernatural*

With respect to faith, what then is the effect of the entitative *habitus* conferred by baptism (or the sacrament of faith) on the being of the recipient? We think that the effect of this grace can be considered, at least under one of its aspects, as giving form to and actualising the soul's capacity to be receptive to the spiritual or supernatural. By virtue of the analogy between every receptive capacity and sensory receptivity, we will call it the *sense of the supernatural*. This definition may give rise to several objections. Is not the supernatural character of grace distorted by comparing it to a capacity that is part of our nature? And does not this capacity, being a 'sense', pertain to the order of powers or faculties of the soul, rather than to the order of being, which would imply its connection to an entitative *habitus*? While we will come back to these questions shortly, we can already provide something of a response by considering the origin of man.

Adam was created in the image of God. Wounded but not destroyed by sin, this theomorphic nature endows man with a being naturally destined to the supernatural life, but completely incapable of realising this spiritual destiny by himself. This theomorphic nature is nevertheless in its essence spirit, which is to say knowledge: man is a creature whose being consists in knowing God – as proved by the true Adam, Jesus Christ, who is the eternal knowledge of the Father.

But, it will be asked, of what use is this spiritual sense in the analysis of faith? Are not intellect and will enough? Our own times have tragically demonstrated that they most certainly are not. For the sense of the supernatural must primarily and essentially result in *the supernatural making sense to me*. The intellect can indeed apply itself to the knowledge of faith; the

---

[4] *Summa Theologiae* IaIIae, 110, 4.

will can indeed want, by a kind of desperate tension, to believe in revelation. But if all this no longer has any *significance* for the believing being, the act of faith is no longer possible. People can only argue about the sex of angels, the nature of monophysitism or the procession of the Holy Spirit if they believe in the existence of these realities, and if such things are meaningful to them and pertain to a conceivable order. We can desire with all our might to give credence to God's word, and to the sacred realities and dogmas which the Church presents to us, only if there is at the very heart of this will (as blind as it may be in the massive intensity of its willing) a trace of intelligibility. But how strong could my will be if these sacred realities *meant absolutely nothing*? I cannot believe in something entirely absurd or impossible. I cannot believe that a circle is a square, that old age precedes infancy, that work does not consume energy, that trees speak or that we can slice water. In one way or another what I believe must say something to me, must be in some manner 'recognisable', however obscure this recognition might be. If the world of faith is totally alien to the believer, how can he continue to believe? And unless the believer experiences within his being, by virtue of a truly spiritual instinct, a kind of connaturality with the world of faith, how can this world be other than totally alien?

Some might object that faith reveals precisely what it is impossible to know by ourselves; this is perfectly correct. But the point of the question lies elsewhere. In the order of sensory knowledge, too, we cannot know *a priori* about the existence of such and such a reality: we need experience to inform us of it. But we admit, or reject, *a priori* the *possibility* of this existence according to our general concept of the physically real. In the same way, only faith reveals the existence of an incarnate and redeeming, dead and resurrected God, but we admit, or reject, *a priori* this *possibility* according to our sense of the metaphysically Real, that is to say according to our sense of the supernatural.

Now, it should be incontestable that the realities in which we ought to believe are of a supernatural order; which is to say that such realities are essentially different from everything we experience in our ordinary and daily life. Hence, to formulate this issue with the perfect clarity required to reveal its full importance: *how can one believe without being a fool?* And this is precisely what the major ideologies of our time, whether Marxism or Freudian psychoanalysis, ask. This is basically the root of Modernism. For contemporary man *religious* faith is a collective neurosis, the infantile mentality of a non-scientific humanity.

3. *The closing of the eye of the heart and the birth of Modernism*

The sense of the supernatural, actualised in our very being, in the essence of the soul, is an effect of the sanctifying grace of baptism. Now baptism is nothing but our sacramental participation in the death and resurrection of Jesus Christ (Rom. 6:3ff.); we are baptised in the Blood of Christ. This salvific immersion is truly a purification: stripping from the baptised person the garment of the 'old man' (Col. 3:9), it lays bare our heart, restores our theomorphic nature and, by the seal or character it stamps on us (II Cor. 1:22), it produces an illumination (Heb. 6:4). This term 'illumination' (*photismos*) was used moreover in sub-apostolic times to designate baptism, the sacrament of the faith. More precisely, this illumination is the purification of the heart, the opening of the eye of the heart, for, according to the promise of Christ, 'the pure in heart ... shall see God' (Mt. 5:8). And St Paul affirms: '[By your faith may] the God of our Lord Jesus Christ ... give you a spirit of wisdom and of revelation in the knowledge of him, having the eyes of your heart *enlightened*' (Eph. 1:15–18), so that we might know, even here below, God's incommensurable greatness, and to what a prodigious state of glory we have been called. And 'man believes with his heart and so is justified' (Rom. 10:10).

We can define the sense of the supernatural then as being *intuitive* by nature: an intuition obscure and imperfect in the bodily state, but one nevertheless true and direct; a nascent sharing in the knowledge that God has of himself, but which must not be considered to be an act of natural reason. More profoundly, it is that light or presentiment which enlightens the will, while the will in its turn guides reason in its movement towards divine truth. This sense is like an almost unconscious intelligence or, more exactly, a *spirit* of knowledge underlying the substance of our volitional and rational soul. By its luminous and cognitive character, this spirit and the objective understanding of faith are of the same nature; by the character of its underlying inherence and instinct for the sacred, this spirit and the subjective willing of the faith are of the same nature. This is what impedes a voluntarist reduction of faith to Protestant fideism, what opposes an intellectualist reduction of faith to some Gnostic deviation. And yet it is the beginning of true Gnosis, the Gnosis spoken of by St Irenaeus and Clement of Alexandria, a stable disposition actualised in the soul's essence by baptismal initiation which goes 'from faith to faith'. In the faith of their hearts all Christians possess this initial and initiatory Gnosis; through it they acquire *the sense of the things of God*, even if they cannot bring this sense to full fruition. It is present in the immensity of the believing multitudes who, for two thousand years, have turned towards the Word and the Cross of Christ, and for whom *the mysteries of the Kingdom*, unveiled in broad daylight and offered to everyone of good will, were not the foolish imaginings, the sickly lucubrations of an Oriental brain or the unconscious projections of the phantasms of a humanity alienated by misery and ignorance, but realities of hope and love.

But as stable and as permanent as this entitative *habitus*, this original intuition of the divine world, may be, it can be lost. Actual graces which superelevate our intellect and will cannot be lost, because we do not possess them. God can send momentary assistance to strengthen our faith or enlighten our intellect with the understanding of a particular dogma. However, he does this only as he judges fit. Even a St Thomas Aquinas, who hesitated over the doctrine of the Immaculate Conception, did not always benefit from a lasting intellectual assistance. And St Theresa of the Child Jesus, during the final years of her life, experienced the most extreme difficulty of will in her acts of faith. But God cannot refuse to enlighten the heart which is open to his grace, that is, to grant to a human being some minimum of intelligibility in the act of faith, lacking which no progress of belief, in either thought or will, would have any meaning. Be that as it may, this initial grace of the sense of the supernatural is only granted to the extent that an individual's heart is open and receptive. And therefore it can be lost, either in part or totally, in proportion to the degree that the human heart closes and hardens. Even when the heart is completely closed, there still remains some reflection of that initial light in the intellect and will, like the glimmer of light which traverses space from a long-vanished star. But this persistence will not last. Soon what was only a reflection, a superstition in the proper sense of the term, a habitude (but no longer a *habitus*), is entirely effaced.

Now what is true for an individual soul is also true for an entire society. For the 'community of persons' is not an empty phrase: there is a community in good as well as in evil. The spirit of an individual is also the spirit of an epoch, and this is not only because of the cultural influence exerted by a civilisation upon its human supports, but also because a *raison d'être* is needed for millions of beings to co-exist within a given time-span. A whole society can completely lose the spirit of faith, the sense of the supernatural, and replace it with a spirit of unbelief. Quite clearly, this is just what has happened over the last two or three centuries in the Christian West. As one can see, what I am saying is quite straightforward. Like every sense, the sense of the supernatural, the original intuition of faith, is the *awareness of a reality*. This is a theme I have explained elsewhere.[5]

Knowledge, be it ever so humble or lofty, is a function of the real. In other words, the supernatural sense of faith is the awareness of a supernatural reality, an imperfect and obscure awareness 'as in a mirror, darkly', but already the 'substance of things hoped for' (Heb. 11:1). It is by means of this sense that humanity 'knows', in the very substance of its being, that everything spoken of in revelation, even though outside the range of our ordinary experience, is *possible*. Without this sense all religious discourse immediately becomes absurd, a debate about the improbable. Now, in point of fact, all the intellectual endeavours of the modern West tend to suggest precisely this: that there is no 'other', and there cannot be any 'other' reality beyond our ordinary experience. This is why, once the Christian conscience succumbs to such suggestions, it produces the heresy

---

[5] Cf. especially *La charité profanée* (Bouère: Editions Dominique Martin Morin, 1979), pp. 123ff.

which Pope St Pius X so accurately labelled 'Modernism'.[6] Such a label for a heresy is unusual, for it designates neither an heresiarch (like Arianism) nor a theological thesis (like docetism); yet it is an accurate one, for in the course of its formation this heresy adopted *in toto* the point of view of the modern world, a point of view wholly defined by the negation of any supernatural reality. I have shown that this negation consists in the closing of the eye of the heart, that ontological root of the act of faith which is the primary and ultimate condition of its possibility in the human order.

As a result, this third type of heresy differs from the others. Attacking the act of faith at its root, the Modernist heresy produces the general condition of all heresies. It is not a determinate heresy, a heresy of either objective or subjective faith. Rather, it is a heresy that involves the very condition that makes any faith possible. It is an ontological or even a metaphysical heresy rather than a religious one, and hence it is, as St Pius X declared in his encyclical *Pascendi* (1907), the 'synthesis or meeting place'[7] of all heresy', a meeting place in both space and time. By providing the only systematic and ordered exposé of Modernism, St Pius X 'recapitulated within it nineteen centuries of Christian divisions'.[8]

Now we are ready to understand what has been happening in the Catholic Church for almost ninety years. For the present crisis, of which the recent Council was the proximate cause, is in reality only the *unfolding* of what was launched in 1902 with the publication of Loisy's *L'Evangile et l'Eglise*, and which, in its inaugural and genuinely intellectual phase, lasted only three or four years. We intentionally use the word 'unfolding' rather than 'revival' or 'reappearance', for, despite the fact that it was forbidden by official Church teaching, combated by a saintly Pope and silenced by the powers of a vigorous ecclesiastical body, Modernism continued to exist in a latent state, for its

---

[6] The term's origin is in fact purely magisterial: cf. E. Poulat, *Histoire du dogme et critique dans la crise moderniste* (Paris: Castermann, 1979), p. 22.

[7] *Translator's note*: The French translation of *Pascendi* uses 'carrefour' here, i.e. 'crossroad' or 'meeting place', while the English translation uses 'synthesis'.

[8] Poulat, *Histoire du dogme*, p. 9.

roots were deeply planted in the modern world and it enjoyed a kind of *de facto* obviousness that was hard to gainsay. After this initial phase of latency, during which it spread throughout the Church, it entered a second phase which was both collective and practical. Leaving the circle of the cognoscenti, it invaded Christian society: both priests and laity; both the teaching and the learning Church, including members of the hierarchy at every level; both professors of dogmatic theology and local pastors. As for its third and present phase – that stemming from its invasive permeation of the Christian social body – it will obviously be just as it was for its first 'hierarch', namely a humanitarian deism hardly distinguishable from a vaguely religious atheism, which I have called 'ideological Christianity'.

Chapter 3

A Brief Aetiology of Modernism

In philosophy, the term 'aetiology' designates the science which intends to seek out the causes of a phenomenon or, more generally, of any reality whatever. Before describing the actual effects of the Modernist crisis in the Christian soul – the inventory of a dead faith – it will be useful to study briefly the causes which have fostered its appearance. Although we may characterise a heresy of the third type on the whole as an atrophy, or even a disappearance, of the sense of the supernatural, we should not forget that this progressive atrophy has had its reasons, and it would be appropriate to say a word about its history.

Two kinds of causes should be envisioned here: those causes external to the Church, tied to the cultural history of the West and its social evolution, and those causes internal to the Church, tied to the state of theological doctrines and to the mentality of the ecclesiastical personnel. Both are obviously attuned to each other and, although we might distinguish between them, we should not separate them. Moreover, we need to observe that these two causal chains concern, as stated above, the entirety of the Christian's being, and not just his thinking or willing. They therefore touch the three dimensions of his being: his body (the spatio-temporal and sensible manifestations of his faith), his soul (his religious life and those feelings associated with it) and lastly his spirit (the doctrine of the faith and the mystical life). It is this aetiological complex that we want to depict.

1. The external causes

We will start with the doctrinal axis, since these matters began there. The truth is that the Catholic Church has been confronted with the most formidable problem that a religion can encounter: the scientific disappearance of the universe of those symbolic forms which let it speak for and manifest itself, that is to say those forms which let it 'exist'. This destruction was effected by Galilean physics; not because, as is ordinarily claimed, it deprived man of his central position[1] – which for St Thomas Aquinas is in any case the least noble and the lowest – but because it reduces the texture of the body, its material substance, to sheer geometry and, by the selfsame stroke, renders this world's ability to serve as a *medium* for the manifestation of God scientifically impossible (or stripped of meaning). The *theophanic* capacity of the world is denied. In an indefinitely extensive and isotropic universe, neither the Incarnation, the Resurrection, nor the Ascension make the least sense. Gone is the sensible basis for the divine and the supernatural. Never had humanity suffered a similar 'epistemological shock', and it has not recovered. Science was thus set up, whether it wanted to be or not, as the enemy of religion. Theology had to proceed, by degrees, with the revision of all its concepts; exegesis was condemned to rank all scriptural data under the category of 'cultural curiosities', 'primitive representations'. One's only choice is between 'demythologising' and 'cultural neurosis', that is to say reducing all of Holy Scripture to a few words of ethical proclamation, or else carrying on as if one believed in events known to be quite impossible.

What did the ecclesial institution do then? It entered resolutely into cultural marginality. It upheld dogma and Scripture against the whole world; it fought, inch by inch, rigorously faithful to the letter of its tradition, imposing more and more vigorously on the faithful (but especially the clergy) the norm and rules of its discipline, yet happy each time a chance concurrence permitted a rejoining of faith and science, above all confident in the hope of an unforeseen reversal of the epistemological situation. But, at the end of the nineteenth century, the Modernist crisis (the present

---

[1] The Copernican system had also done so, without for all that giving rise to the least reproach from Pope Paul III, who accepted the dedication of *De revolutionibus orbium cœlestium*. I have studied this question at length in *La crise du symbolisme religieux* (Lausanne: L'Age d'Homme, 1990), pp. 19–132.

crisis being only an extension and generalisation of that one), smouldering since Galileo, finally ignited.

Why Modernism, and at that moment? Here we encounter the second and third axes of religious existence, which define on the one hand its life-style (its life-rhythms, sentiments, feasts, joys and sorrows), and on the other the physical setting of its spatio-temporal unfolding. Those clerics who 'colonised' the world of ideas suffered the earthquakes of Galileo and Spinoza which shook that world, but the life of the people continued to unfold according to the rhythms of nature and in a scantily geometrised world. Up until the end of the nineteenth century, the majority of the French population remained peasants. Up until the end of the nineteenth century, the rational universe of science remained without technical proof to the eyes of a humanity which still lived by the 'mystery' of nature, where everything is possible. This is why, for the vast majority of seventeenth- and eighteenth-century Christians, the chief concern remained *human life* much more profoundly than the superficial disorder and discontinuity of historical events, human life in the succession of its ages from birth to death, which the liturgy made its own responsibility, and to which it alone gave meaning by connecting it vertically to the divine, which might burst in at any moment. Man lived in dialogue with God because there was, after all, nothing more important. But, with the French Revolution, politico-social temporality progressively hemmed in human existence. Human life lost its individuality. It was normalised by an all-encompassing temporality, that of *humanity in progress*, which went beyond particular destinies 'into the future', unravelling the cycles of life and transforming them into insular segments of an indefinite chain. Human history enclosed itself then within its own horizon; God no longer had anything to do with it; one does not halt progress. As a result, religion – in other words the liturgy and morality (Sunday masses, feasts and celebrations of the yearly cycle, baptisms, marriages, funerals, the commandments of God and Friday abstinence) – religion, we say, appeared more and more foreign to 'real life'. Between labour unrest, the exercising of the right to vote, democratic enthusiasms and the siren-song of things to come, baptisms and solemn Holy Communions were hardly of any interest.

In a parallel way, finally, and from the viewpoint of the spatio-temporal setting, we were witness to a prodigious transformation of our 'living space'. And since then there has been an undeniable increase in technology, so that now the mechanical order holds sway over the world and bespeaks only the power of man, the efficiency of matter, producing the most surprising and marvellous effects with the help of the most simple and obvious means. Everywhere it impresses upon us that everything is done by movement, impact and the meshing of gears, that there is no mystery to things, and that industry is master of an entirely manufacturable reality.

With all of this, then, what we call the *sense of the supernatural* has disappeared from the human heart, that sense which from the beginning of time kept faithful vigil in our immortal souls, awaiting its illumination by a divine revelation, that sense thanks to which the supernatural could make sense, that eye which looked with unwearied hope for a 'beyond' of heaven and earth, that humble desire for a Paradise which gave a presentiment of itself through all the beauty of the world, that belief within us, at the root of all faith, that not everything is here in front of our eyes, that not all is said, that all is still possible, that angels watch over us, that Mary protects us – in short, that God loves us . . . It is this which is dead, overwhelmed by the din of engine noise and crushed beneath the pall of urban concrete.

Such is the snare in which our religion was caught; it calls itself the modern world. A terrible and effective snare, because incontestable as a mountain, and because we can do nothing about it. Doubtless this conclusion seems quite pessimistic. And yet is there another conclusion so apt to clarify this strange prophecy of Christ, so apt to give plausibility to its coming true: 'Nevertheless, when the Son of man comes, will he find faith on earth?' (Lk. 18:8)? Have we truly asked ourselves under what conditions it might become meaningful? Do we imagine that our good will alone is brought into play in faith? That the truth of Christ will always be clearly set before us for our commitment, men being distracted from paying attention to it only by the multitude of those earthly preoccupations which entice them? But there would be nothing here to deceive 'even the elect themselves'! And they rest secure in the conviction that faith is only a subjective (and therefore changing) disposition faced with a doctrinal content immutable in its proposals. But what happens is much more serious and inevitably leads to placing the faith in a state of near-impossibility; that is, into such a state that, should a man have the will to believe and commit himself, everything would transpire as if he no longer had the ability to do so. Judge for yourself. Objectively, in what concerns Holy Scripture and dogma, modern hermeneutics proceeds with such a critique regarding the form and content of the expressions of our faith that we are quite simply no longer able to discern or recognise the *sense* of the sacred deposit. This exegesis does not intend to demonstrate the physical unreality of the Incarnation or the Ascension, but only intends to show that our intelligence does not, in fact, know what it is thinking when trying to imagine these mysteries, and therefore that they truly have no objective significance. Subjectively, on the other hand, scientifico-materialist suggestion is so strong that the producing of an attitude of religious belief by a human subject can be experienced by that same subject as a genuine insanity. That religion might be a 'collective neurosis' is not just a Freudian theory, it is also the solid conviction of modern reason, the overwhelming presence of which ends up neutralising the least wish to commit oneself to an invisible Transcendent.

Such are, I think, the positive causes which make the appearance of the Modernist heresy in the very bosom of the Church almost inevitable. Essentially a crisis of the clergy, because only churchmen could at the same time become suddenly aware of the 'epistemological' impossibility of traditional faith on the one hand, and, on the other, of the need for a radical transformation of the very substance of religion, if one were to attempt to save what could be saved. For, we should not forget, this was the chief concern of the Loisys, the Turmels, the Héberts and the Tyrrells. It was quite necessary that the 'predicament of the faith', both objectively and subjectively, seem truly untenable in order for the especially knowledgeable and reflective clergy to think it necessary to renounce their 'voluntary blindness' and, willy-nilly, draw for religion itself those conclusions which seemed obvious to them. The magisterium's response to the casting of doubt on everything by Modernism was in conformity with the rule of faith: uphold the entirety of dogma, banish the guilty, constrain the hesitant, watch everyone and impose the Anti-Modernist Oath. So why, under these conditions, did the Church experience the most serious crisis of her history fifty years later with the opening of Vatican II? Why did religious history suddenly stop unfolding in the direction defined by the Tridentine Church, a direction confirmed by Vatican I and in no way abolished by Vatican II? Why in a few years has it tottered into the pillaging of the liturgy, revolt against the magisterium, abandonment of the most basic dogmas, and even apostasy? And this, not only on the part of some theologians, but on the part of numerous priests and even some bishops? Here we must look into what we have called the internal causes.

2. *The internal causes*

The first or chief cause of the post-conciliar revolution resides in the actual losing, in the very bosom of the Church, of the anti-Modernist battle and Modernism's apparent victory; so that it is often the members of the clergy, at least the most active and intelligent of them, who have become, willingly or not, the authors of Modernist propaganda. Professors of Holy Scripture and theologians publicly submitted to the condemnation of heresy, but the real causes weighed so heavily on their minds that their intellectual convictions as scholars or thinkers could hardly be changed. How many of them, with the proclamation of the dogma of the Assumption, believed that Mary with her glorious body was truly raised into heaven?

A second series of causes sprang from the appearance, within the Church and in the laity, of a strong current which its adversaries called fundamentalism and which contributed not a little, by its law-and-order theological literalism, its obsessive inquisitorial mentality and its taste for denunciations, to provoking an uncontrollable backlash, not only on the part of the Modernists, which is only too obvious, but also on the part of the 'moderate' clergy, that is to say the immense majority of priests – a reaction which, aided by the succession of generations, also ended up being shared even by the senior hierarchy. This reaction which exploded at Vatican II shot back the bolt of a magisterium taken unawares, swept all before it and seemed to carry away two thousand years of tradition in its universal devastation. Certainly the 'fundamentalists' were often right as to doctrine, exegesis, morality and liturgy, but – and this is the least one can say – they did not know how to make themselves understood. Not only – the world being 'modern' – did the Modernists continue to be violently driven toward the destruction of tradition, but also the face of truth presented by its defenders turned them invincibly away from it, given their untenable scorn for metaphysics and speculative orthodoxy. This was not the result anticipated by 'fundamentalist Catholics', but this was nevertheless the outcome. These Catholics believed overmuch that they were the proprietors of the truth and that truth was to be identified with its formulation (which does not mean that the traditional formulations should be changed, but only that in every formulation there is something of the inexpressible, by which it escapes every human attempt at appropriation). However that may be, the highest and most noble end cannot be indifferent to the means used.

Lastly, there is a third kind of internal cause which was connected to the state of theological science at that time: we mean the rebirth of Thomism starting with the encyclical *Æterni Patris* of 4 August 1879. By establishing the doctrine of the Common Doctor as a norm for the philosophical and theological sciences, Leo XIII rendered a most eminent service to the Church. But he also provided in advance a caution about the excesses of a neo-Thomism which might attempt to reduce Thomas's metaphysics to some theses duly authorised and organised in order to impose their teaching everywhere, not hesitating to correct St Thomas himself when he strayed. Now this school of thought held to the Aristotelian rationality reviewed and corrected by Cajetan, a school mindful of not falling under the blow of the Kantian critique: it posed in principle a radical distinction between the order of natural knowledge and that of supernatural knowledge. By this it denied the naturally supernatural dimension of the intellect, which St Thomas however had indubitably taught: 'for him, the whole divine mystery is already present in the very nature of the intellect.'[2] Moreover we know the ostracism which befell the future Cardinal de Lubac after the publication of his book *Surnaturel* and the indirect condemnation which it earned him (1950: *Humani Generis*). Beyond these sad events, we need to remember that, by separating the intellectual from the spiritual, this neo-Thomism condemned theological work to be nourished exclusively by reasoning, thus cutting it off from the most vital of its roots, its mystical root. Basically it wanted to combat Modernism with Modernism's own weapons: without being aware of it, it had already conceded defeat.

The response demanded by the Modernist crisis should have been the elaboration of a *theology of culture*, chiefly in its sacral and religious forms, since it is these that are the irrefutable witnesses to the presence within us of a sense of the supernatural. Was Thomism capable of providing it? I doubt it. Anyway, to see only a profane rationality in human nature transforms it into an abstraction which has had a *cultural* existence only in post-Cartesian European philosophy.

---

[2] E. Gilson, *Letters of Etienne Gilson to Henri de Lubac* (San Francisco: Ignatius Press, 1988), letter of 21 June 1965, p. 95. Likewise p. 82, where he speaks of the 'synchronous, but not identically-related, natural and supernatural character of this natural desire to see God'.

Chapter 4

Inventory of a Dead Faith

1. *From the destruction of nature to a nature shut up within itself*

Now that I have sketched the historical circumstances to some extent, I come to a more general and more typological consideration of the unfolding of heresy in the course of modern times down to our own day.

The first thing to be understood is the link that leads us from the second to the third type of heresy – from Protestantism to Modernism. That one follows upon the other is obvious.

Solicitude for the honour of God haunted Luther's heart and led him, as we have seen, into a kind of radical supernaturalism: the more one humbles human nature, the more one exalts the Creator and Redeemer. Any admixture of the least particle of humanity in the divine order or the work of justification is, for Luther, an unbearable blasphemy that unleashes his fury. This is why the papist Mass, which confers on the priest the power to act *in persona Christi* to accomplish a real sacrifice, is not only an abomination, but the supreme sacrilege. This is also why his entire reform can be reduced to an unremitting effort to erase those elements of human nature whose presence the Catholic Church consecrates in all her rites and teachings. 'Faith alone' and 'Scripture alone', which he claims as principles, are in fact functions of the principle 'God alone'. 'It is strictly necessary', he writes, 'to distinguish between God's virtue and our own, between the work of God and our own, if we wish to live piously . . . this is the *only* question *in the entire sum of Christian things* in which consists and on which are hung at the same time the knowledge of ourselves and the knowledge and honour of God.'[1] Moreover, it is not only man who is 'completely corrupt in his nature',[2] so that there is nothing good in him, but also nature, which is for Luther totally foreign to the divine order. Hence nothing in nature can serve as *matter* for sacramental works. Baptismal water and its consecration, as well as sacramentals, candles, palms, bells and all forms of papist 'prestidigitation', are condemned.

The basic nature of the Protestant revolt is clearly visible in these opinions: it is an angelism.[3] It denies the immanence of the Uncreated in the created. It destroys all of the bodily forms of the sacred. Jealous for the honour of God, Luther did not understand that the majesty of the Absolute can accept both the goodness of the relative and its worthiness to co-operate with divine grace. At the same time, to the extent that nature for him is no longer a locus for grace, since it is no longer *essentially* destined to the glory of deification, it gains its own autonomy and becomes the locus of technical and industrial activity. In contrast to this, Catholic (and Orthodox) teaching holds that Creation retains in its depths something of paradisal nature, and its purely profane and mercantile use violates the essential sacredness of the cosmos. It is this that explains the economic superiority of Anglo-Saxon countries.

As a result of this radical negation of the theomorphic capacity of the creature, the sense of the supernatural, which was available to human nature under the effect of divine grace, becomes impossible. In this way human nature, with its independence and its limitations, becomes closed in upon itself. Supernaturalised nature disappears and gives way to a nature that is entirely and solely natural, consigned to domination and exploitation by an utterly profane world. The waters of grace

---

[1] Cf. *On the Bondage of the Will* in Christiani (trans.), *Luther tel qu'il fut* (Paris: Fayard, 1955), p. 138.

[2] Cf. *Articles of Schmalkald*, ibid., p. 196.

[3] Angelism is in essence the sin of the most angelic of angels, Lucifer. Lucifer revolted against God because *he did not understand* that God is able to create a being as remote from the divine splendour as man, and that he is even able to become incarnate in him. The infra-angelic creation appeared to Lucifer as unworthy of the transcendence of the Principle. Appointing himself guardian of God's honour against God himself, he bestows on himself the mission of removing the taint of human creation from the pure mirror of the celestial universe, the mission of destroying it and of preventing its redemption in glory.

cannot penetrate a nature that is purely human, that is sealed off and shut up within itself.[4]

From the very moment that this sense of the supernatural is lost, the entire universe of revelation becomes inconceivable and quite literally *impossible*. And yet, although latent, an awareness of this sense remains in the Christian soul, revealing itself only little by little. Most certainly 'God is dead' – and it is not by chance that this 'death' was first achieved in eighteenth-century Protestant Germany,[5] before being explicitly formulated by Nietzsche. But it escapes notice in two ways. First, as regards Protestant subjectivity, faith, identified with the *sentiment* of faith, is psychologically nourished by its own affirmation, drawing from this the satisfaction and assurance which it no longer wishes to extract from an intellectual intuition of the supernatural. Secondly, as regards the Catholic community, faith, identified with the love of humanity, is nourished ideologically by the spectacle of one's own goodness. Here we have, despite everything, only simulacra of a faith which would be unable to hide its progressive wasting away were it not at the same time busying itself with 'altering religion' – with erasing from dogma, liturgy, Scripture and morality those objective guidelines likely to make so radical a mutation conspicuous. However, this erasure of the faith's objective guidelines is itself only an effect of the mutation which it has helped to disguise. It is possible – for those Christian souls who have become strangers to their own religion – only to the extent that the religious universe surrounding them no longer has any meaning, or at least no longer has the meaning attributed to it by Tradition. And if, perchance, someone remains committed, this is most often by force of habit or by a residual psychological affinity.

---

[4] Our description is schematic. The concrete reality is necessarily different or Protestantism would in no way be a Christianity. Despite what has been said, Protestantism must remain faithful to the most basic inspiration of its founder and to the strength of his mystical instinct. Luther was, in some respects, a giant in comparison to contemporary Modernists, who seem more like amoebas. Nevertheless, even though it would be false to deny Luther's faith in Christ, the fact remains that by wholly excluding human nature from all co-operation with grace, he has to some extent made the mediation of the Redeemer an impossibility (or inconceivable).

[5] As has been clearly shown by Jean-Marie Paul in his *Dieu est mort en Allemagne: des Lumières à Nietzsche* (Paris: Payot, 1994).

2. *Modernism has lost the key to the religious heart of man*

Thus we become more and more aware, through the stages of its atrophy, of the need to grant that, at the core of the human being, there is a natural capacity for an ordering toward the supernatural. The example of Lutheran supernaturalism imposes this on us.

The fundamental principle of Catholic theology on this topic is, we repeat, that grace does not destroy nature, but perfects it. Now clearly the sense of the supernatural, which, when present, is a fruit of divine grace, corresponds to a possibility inherent in our nature. But the state of pure nature is only an abstraction. As St Thomas informs us (*Summa Theologiae* Ia, 95, 1), man was created in a state of grace, a state of grace which allowed him to accomplish and realise that to which his theomorphic nature was ordained. For, after all, it should not be forgotten that man was created in the image and likeness of God. Even though the original Fall caused man to lose his state of grace, it could not annihilate his theomorphic essence without destroying man as such. Thus after the Fall a theomorphic possibility endured within his wounded nature, the memory of a spiritual destiny awaiting fulfilment. And this memory is truly a natural capacity for the supernatural, a capacity impotent and formless in itself, but nevertheless real, and the means by which man is distinguished from the animals. Grace comes specifically to endow this natural capacity for the supernatural with form, by opening it to the saving truths of faith and rendering it efficacious. 'Create in me a clean heart, O God,' sings the Psalmist, 'and put a new and right spirit within me' (Ps. 50:10). Thus grace comes to fulfil the hopes of nature; but, because God always gives more than we ask, this fulfilment infinitely surpasses all of our expectations.

Further, if it were not for this natural capacity for the supernatural, it would be impossible to account for the fact that everywhere on earth we find the presence of religion, which is to say the affirmation of an invisible reality and the accomplishing of acts which make it possible to enter into contact with it. True, this capacity is actualised and given form only through revelation, which implies that by itself this capacity is unable to gain access to the supernatural (just as the eye on its own is unable to produce light), and may atrophy and disappear if not exercised by the light of faith. There is then a discontinuity from the one to the other, from form-giving grace to natural capacity. Even though grace may perfect nature, it initially presents itself as something other than and transcendent to nature, because what nature is ignorant of, grace realises for it. Nature does not truly know itself, and its conscious needs do not correspond to the real requirements of its essence. This is why the first step of this natural capacity for the supernatural should be an act of *obedience* and the renunciation of any vague awareness that nature might have of itself. This is in fact why such an ability was conferred by God on our nature, allowing it to correspond to grace with a view to its realising its destiny to glory; this ability is called the 'obediential potency', or the capacity for obedience.[6] Therefore, it is not at the beginning but at the end that man perceives that faith truly provides answers to those questions which he asks himself, and this because the questions themselves have been transformed.

It is this free act of obedience that Modernism refuses to make. And, with this selfsame act, the door to the human heart is closed. We said above that the Modernists are strangers to the objective world of faith. We now see that they are strangers to their own theomorphic nature. What Modernism no longer comprehends, and for this reason wishes to destroy, is not only the dogmas and rites binding us to God, but also the human essence made in the image of God, which defines our destiny and is expressed in our will to believe. Even the Lutheran faith becomes inaccessible to it.

3. *Faith has become nothing more than its own historical manifestation*

What then is left of faith, and why do the Modernists not become complete atheists? This question is not easily answered. I will simply say that complete atheism raises as many difficulties for the Modernist as does the traditional faith. Not difficulties of the metaphysical order, for nothing is more foreign to

---

[6] We are leaving aside the theological discussions on the nature of this 'obediential potency' and seeing it in its mystical prototype, the Blessed Virgin Mary. In essence we should turn to the teaching of St Basil quoted by St Gregory Nazianzus: 'Man is a creature who has received the commandment to become God'; cf. p. 134, n. 12.

Modernism than metaphysics, but difficulties on the psychological and historical level, in short on the human level: what do they make of the universal presence of religiosity observed by the historian, and can they take away all significance from such an important part of human life? Would not this truly be a mutilation of human life?[7]

But the reason for Modernism's strict refusal to embrace atheism provides us with a key to its attitude towards faith, and this is the issue which ties together all of our themes for reflection. As already noted, Protestantism reduces orthodoxy to orthopraxy; that is, orthopraxy fulfils the requirements of orthodoxy so that, despite everything, orthodoxy still remains a possibility. In point of fact, orthopraxy is the outer boundary of orthodoxy, since, for orthopraxy, the *content of faith is faith itself*. Faith in doctrine becomes the doctrine of faith. And, by virtue of this same *praxis* become theoretical content, Protestantism deems itself established as an anti-Catholic Church (in the same sense that we speak of antimatter in physics). Such is not the attitude of Modernism. The loss of the sense of the supernatural makes all doctrinal judgements, all affirmations of the dogmas of faith meaningless (whereas the Lutheran *Credo* hardly differs from its Catholic counterpart). Strictly speaking, they have no conceivable object. So what is left? Only the subjective step of faith. And indeed Protestantism has taught this principle to Modernism. But there is an enormous difference. For the Modernist this subjective step of the believing will is no longer seen as a dogma. It is stripped of the doctrinal value attributed to it by Luther, which is to say of its supernatural import, of the demand expressed within it for an order from on high, the accomplishment of which would have value as a real sign of the Transcendent.[8] Seen in this light, Modernism is simply taking Protestantism literally. Since human nature is completely foreign to the supernatural order, why should a subjective act of the will to believe escape this rule? And why should this subjective act be the sole means of situating ourselves in the divine? Faith, then, is reduced to a form of human behaviour,

---

[7] Here we are not far from the Kantian God, a 'postulate of practical reason'.

[8] I have dealt with this question in *La crise du symbolisme religieux* (Lausanne: L'Age d'Homme, 1990).

and the truths of faith are only some of its products; while, for the believing consciousness, religious behaviour is only the visible aspect of an invisible reality, which is both its true meaning and its most important aspect. For the Modernist consciousness, *all* faith is reduced to religious behaviour. In short, Christian faith is the history of faith in Christ, which is itself but an entirely historical reality. And here the basic 'theological position' of Modernism becomes obvious. From this principle flows *all* of its exegetical assertions and its contemporary pseudo-theologies. According to Modernism, the Gospels set down in writing the first religious 'constructs' of a Christian consciousness by reacting to the historical facts of the preaching and death of Christ; while the ensuing dogmatic declarations were only a succession of other constructs, engendered either by continuity or reaction out of variations in religious consciousness.

It is clear that Loisy proceeds by this means to a kind of identification of history as science (or historiography) with history as reality of the human past. In reducing Christian faith to the history of Christian behaviour, he reduces it to what the historians can observe. But to do so begs the question, for only an *a priori* philosophy of history could ever justify such a step. According to Loisy, a thousand reasonings are as nothing compared to the fact of a single grain of wheat.[9] What Loisy does not understand is that what matters here is the one thousand and first reason; facts themselves are such only as a function of some theoretical point of view which isolates and determines them. By itself a grain of wheat proves absolutely nothing. In reading Loisy it becomes clear that he is a total stranger to all metaphysical speculation, and that this philosophical incapacity of his is not an advantage – it is a defect and a failing.

4. *The Church is only an historical form of religious consciousness*

Religious agnosticism and the idea that all knowledge is relative go hand in hand. Once one denies the sense of the supernatural (or denies the possibility of believing that a supernatural reality

---

[9] Cf. E. Poulat, *Histoire du dogme et critique dans la crise moderne* (Paris: Castermann, 1979), p. 186.

can exist), one also denies the ontological value of cognitive statements, for these two are interdependent. Or, if one prefers, ontology and theology are intertwined. Here as elsewhere the order of grace perfects the natural order by surpassing it. That human consciousness can go out from itself and deal with objective reality in some way finds its complete and more than perfect model in the act of faith by which being, coming from without and revealing itself, is welcomed into the intellect. Far from being opposed to intellectual knowledge, revelation provides it with an unsurpassable and fulfilling norm. Faith is the truth of knowledge. All of human knowledge aspires, without attaining it, to this revelation which is realised by faith and by means of which Reality itself is made known to the intellect. What poet, what scholar, what philosopher has not dreamed of a knowledge that would be the very being of things, the *logos*, the revealing word which would speak directly to him? And if, when this happens, our intellect is clouded, it is not because of the Object's obscurity, but rather because its light is too intense for the capacities of our fallen intellect. Conversely, and from the human side, the very possibility of dogmatic statements depends upon the ability of our intellect to perceive being. The Divine Sun can indeed reveal itself to blind eyes, provided they are first healed of their blindness; but it would in no way reveal itself to sightless beings. Thus – and Modernism provides us with the experimental proof – the loss of the sense of the supernatural is but the religious aspect of the loss of the sense of the ontological, or the intuition of being, and vice versa.

Under these circumstances Modernism was and still is incapable of establishing a new Church, in other words a new *community of faith*; its 'principles' preclude such an outcome. A community of faith specifically implies that, on the one hand, any speculative statement can have an ontological bearing, and, on the other, that a speculative religious statement may hold an objective meaning for relative and historic man. Besides, the establishment of a new Church is useless. The Church, as it exists at the present time, is itself, from the Modernist point of view, a product of history. It is the form that human faith in Christ has assumed at this time. It is a fact. Yet it does not really have the value or significance that it attributes to itself.

And, above all, it has come to a point in its history when it must renounce attributing a transcendent and divine significance to itself. This significance is not false in so far as it expresses the religious consciousness of an epoch, but it is an historical fact and nothing more. There is a glaring disparity between the way in which the Church regards itself and the times in which we live. It is this awareness that needs to be changed, by adapting the Church to the truth of its historic situation. In default of this it will disappear. Neither Loisy nor the new theologians wish to destroy the Church. Quite the opposite. They have come forward to save it. Loisy's most serene and deeply rooted conviction was that 'whatever may have been said, I did not write to disquiet those believers who do not know, but to reassure those who do.'[10] Not without a certain sadness we see this great scholar – but one with a crippled understanding – imperturbably unwinding the skein of his discourse, without perceiving that he no longer understands what he is talking about.

Certainly the tone changes with the Küngs or the Drewermanns, and present disputes are more radical in appearance. But this is basically the same doctrine and the same atrophy of the sense of the supernatural. They too deny any ontological import for dogmas which, in themselves and as a momentary expression of religious consciousness, have no truth but the historical. To counter them with such and such a truth which they seem to deny would only be wasted effort. They deny no article of faith; they only enquire into its significance for present-day consciousness and declare it null. One can condemn them, but in doing so the Church would only prove that it has understood nothing of their point of view. They are not combating one (objective) faith with another. They are searching for ways to express how one can 'be Christian' today. For it is Christian 'being' that is called into question, in so far as the sense of the supernatural concerns our being, and precisely in so far as the man of today is destitute of it. As long as the sense of the supernatural is present, one can indeed raise the issue of Christian knowledge or Christian action, but not of being itself. And yet to ask oneself, as some do, what the

---

[10] Cf. *Autour d'un petit livre*, 2nd edn. (Paris: A. Picard, 1903), p. 258.

attributing of this adjective *Christian* to a *being* might mean, one must in fact no longer possess within oneself this *entitative habitus*, this eye of the heart open to the supernatural light of glory.

5. *Divine grace is forgotten*

The almost complete disappearance of the sense of the supernatural is marked, in the work of these 'theologians', by the parallel absence of what is nevertheless essential to Christian life: divine grace. This absence has gone curiously unnoticed. Everything transpires as if their theses have monopolised our attention because of their novelty or their scandalous character. Some praise them, some, to their secret amusement, reproach them. Their condemnation is the object of many debates and provides the chance for some journalists to raise the spectre of the Inquisition; in short they are in the spotlight. But no one seems to notice that we find, in their works, nothing of the *acting presence* of the one person essential for 'Christian being', or for the 'inner life', without which all of this would not have the least significance: the person of God himself. God is not there; does not intervene, and plays no part whatsoever. When we read them, we discover that for them everything is played out on a purely human level, between today's needs and the religious consciousness inherited from the past, between a living humanity and a faith reputedly sclerotic, between the idea which should be formed of Christianity in our own times and that formed in times gone by. We *never* leave the human order. And yet, as St Paul tells us in Acts 17:28, 'in him we live and move and have our being'; which means that being Christian is a being-in-God, beginning here and now. But they no longer understand this.

This is why it is so hard to dispute any of their theses, or to undertake a general refutation: they deny the tribunal of doctrine in itself. By virtue of their extra-dogmatic point of view and their basic agnosticism, they see in any given dogma only a passing moment in the history of religious consciousness, a by-product of economic alienation or an unconscious repression of the libido. Without doubt one should never surrender all claims to such a dialectic-based refutation, on the one hand because there is no other way to defend the truth, and on the other because it honours the presence of reason in those being refuted, even if it does not cure them. But we should not forget, for all that, that the 'Christians' to whom it is addressed are so in name only. What do they want, basically, and what is their intended goal? They tell us the answer openly: to substitute the *humanisation* of man for his *divinisation*. Such a programme is effectively a condemnation of the human being, who is found to be reduced to his or her own limits, to a death-haunted contingency: to an absence of rejoicing and hope which scorches our lungs with the dismal breath of hell. What speaks to us in such a language is a veritable death-wish: it is what the blind have collected to prove to the last of those who see that light does not exist.

6. *An established Modernism?*

The result of such an evolution is not easy to describe. The spread of the Modernist heresy is now hardly contestable. So commonplace has it become that its most excessive and most provocative forms have lost their power to subvert. Also one cannot sustain oneself indefinitely at the same pitch of revolutionary exaltation: after periods of upheaval, clearly a new and settled order is needed, an order situated, however, on a theological level well below the previous one.

Has the bedrock of traditional faith vanished from the whole of the Catholic body? Certainly not. The resistance of this body to Modernist propaganda, through divine grace and natural inertia, is greater than anticipated by its promoters. For the Christian people to admit, moreover, that the truth of yesteryear, taught in the catechism, is no longer today's truth, they would have to give themselves up to questionings of a philosophical and theological nature (not to mention those raised by the social sciences), which, by definition, they are incapable of, and which would be, even for an experienced intellectual, something akin to tightrope-walking. We are witnessing, therefore, a slowing in the spread of Modernism: on the one hand, as we mentioned, it has of itself lost some of its steam, and on the other, it penetrates the Christian sphere less and less easily to the extent that it reaches the densest strata of faith. This represents the stabilisation of a situation 'schizoid' by nature: on one side is a clergy which, in its 'advanced' factions, pursues its own intellectual and cultural modernisation, ejecting a share of Christian dogmas by no means negligible, demythologising Scripture (no more Annunciation, Magi, temptation in the wilderness, multiplication of bread, Transfiguration, Ascension, etc.), striving to transform the celebrations of the Eucharist into the congregation's celebration of itself; on the other is the faithful (what is left of them!), generally submissive and obedient, who continue for better or worse to practise their religion, and who quite simply do not succeed in coming to any clear awareness of the frequently Modernist character of the doctrine taught or the liturgies imposed. This is an unexpected state of affairs for post-Conciliar revolutionaries.

But, for twenty years, another factor has intervened in the process I am describing; something that neither the strategy of the reformers nor that of the traditionalists had foreseen: the arrival in the chair of St Peter of an exceptional pope, who is undertaking, with a steadfast obstinacy and without denying the Second Vatican Council, the mending of Christian unity through a return to the unity of faith, which he has called a 'new evangelisation'. The most notable event in this pontificate, a pontificate providential in many respects, has been the publication of the *Catechism of the Catholic Church*, where the entirety of a most orthodox faith is found to be made explicit. This is an essential work because it stands as a visible point of reference, a norm declared and recognisable to everyone, and because, by this very fact, it judges and allows to be judged all expressions of faith. The strategy of this pope has not been to denounce or to issue disciplinary condemnations of the various forms of heresy or their spokesmen (with a few rare exceptions, and setting aside the case of Mgr Lefèbvre, which does not stem from heresy). His strategy was and still is to mend the Christian fabric in the very locales of its existence, to attempt to 'occupy terrain' by confirming his brothers in the faith, to rebuild the Church starting with its most ancient spiritual centres: Santiago de Compostela, Mont Sainte-Odile, the sanctuary of Czestochowa, Fulda, etc.

By this fact, the worldly quarrel perpetuated by Modernists and anti-Modernists in the closed field of the Church is found to be relativised with respect to a third party – the Roman

Inventory of a Dead Faith

Pontiff, powerfully seconded by Cardinal Ratzinger. The magisterium is no longer torn, as in Paul VI's time, between rival factions that he supported and contended with by turns; it has set to work on a project of vast proportions: the evangelisation of our former Christendom, a project with respect to which the two rival parties have been constrained to situate themselves, and which they see – O paradox! – only as an intrusion. This is why establishment Modernism has developed, with respect to John Paul II, in the universal Church which it occupies unduly, a rightly pathological hatred; while the 'schismatics' of Ecône have been reduced to ruminating over some inconsistent grievances, some doctrinal scraps fallen from the papal table which, with their flair for infallibility, they judge to be poisoned.

Such appears to be the present state of affairs. Whatever its outcome might be, it is certain that the intervention of the present pope in the history of the Church invites faithful Catholics of Tradition to a revision of attitude. By calling them to the task of recovery in which he has been involved, he is showing that henceforth it is not absurd to carry on this struggle from *within* the Church. A supreme ruse, some will say. But in order to decide, or at least shed some light on our decision, there is no other means than to proceed with a critical examination of the very notion of spiritual resistance. Up until now I have described the different stages in the eclipsing of our sense of the supernatural, because this was the best way to bring us to an awareness of its presence within us and therefore to fight against its disappearance. But every strategy for resistance includes a risk, a risk we ignore at our peril: the risk of losing sight of the very reasons for which this posture of resistance was adopted.

Chapter 5

Spirit and Resistance

The art of spiritual resistance is a most difficult one. By resisting, in the name of the spirit, those forms and forces which seem to menace it, not only do we risk passing for dull, habit-bound reactionaries, which is nothing, but also sincerely deceiving ourselves in combat – confusing the resistance of the spirit with the spirit of resistance, and thus irremediably compromising the cause which we wished to defend. Under what conditions can the fight for the spirit avoid sinning against the spirit? This is what we will attempt to explain. Starting with an analysis of the concept of resistance, showing next how the spirit is, of itself, the only true resistance, we will see, lastly, how Tradition provides us with the model and secret of spiritual resistance, for, with this, spirit becomes resistance and resistance is transformed into spirit.

1. Fidelity to principle, resistance to history

To begin with, let us see what each of the three roots of the word 'resistance' might teach us. The primary root in the formation of this term comes last and is derived from the Latin *sto, stare*, which indicates the fact of standing erect, of being held upright in a specific place. This involves, then, the most elementary form of existence, for to exist here below is first of all to be 'there', to be localised at a given point in space. The reduplication *si-sto, sistere*, forming the second root, indicates not only the quite physical fact of staying in one place, but also the fact of stopping there and hence of occupying it, of inhabiting it, of being truly there where one is, of establishing oneself there and remaining there. Here, time has been added to space: *sistere* prolongs in the duration of a life what was previously seen only under its mode of spatial determination. The third root, the prefix *re-*, indicates return, repetition; it introduces a new idea, for one only returns, one only comes back from whence one has departed, and, since this involves a return to a *sistere*, i.e. a return to a place in which one had been established, it must therefore be because one had been chased from it, or at least ran the risk of being dislodged from it. *Resistere* is not, then, simply a maintaining or a permanence, not only a 'remaining', but the active rejection of an imposed displacement. With *resistere*, one's temporal dwelling-place becomes involved with an external and invasive reality. We see by this that resistance is not primary, like *stare* or *sistere*. It is a reaction, a response, but of a particular kind, for it consists solely in keeping to the first state. It is the first state which is itself the response that resistance secondarily opposes to dislodging forces. Resistance as such, then, does not seem to have its principle within itself: it is a dislodging force which transforms maintenance, *sistere*, into resistance. And yet the principle, the *raison d'être* of resistance, cannot be anything but this very maintenance.

Such is the paradox of resistance, or at least its basic difficulty: it is a pressure to dislodge that gives rise to resistance; but what resistance wants is existence to continue as it was prior to the dislodging pressure, in other words, continuity of life. Now precisely by the very fact of this pressure to dislodge, what is resisting can no longer be purely and simply that which was subsisting. For subsistence is the natural and spontaneous exercise of the act of existing. It is the will to be oneself, not an active refusal to be anybody else; while to refuse to be other than oneself is to will one's own essence actively, to counter what is menacing one's existence. And this will involves two consequences. With the first, that essence to which one intends to remain faithful may cease being the immanent principle of that human being's activity, may cease being that principle which spontaneously and naturally animates it. This essence almost becomes then a transcendent principle, a norm or idea toward which the human being feels duty-bound, and from which, as a consequence, he almost spontaneously differentiates himself. With the second consequence this transcendent principle, this norm or ideal, whose servant man in his resistance feels himself to be, must not only be maintained, but also defended, which presupposes the setting up of a protective apparatus as effective as possible: in short, the servant is also a guardian and a sentinel. These two points will now be considered.

The will to resist, as I have said, introduces, between a human being and the inspiring principle to which he is remaining faithful, a distance which causes a loss of immediacy for this principle's inspiring activity. Nevertheless, it is truly for the sake of its value, for the sake of its inspiring virtue that this principle should be preserved. But, from this moment, does not resistance begin to deprive one of enjoying the benefit which it wants to safeguard?

Consider the case of the *ancien régime* or the former liturgy. If, for some, the status quo, which political or liturgical revolution has rendered 'ancient', should be preserved, and if it is right to resist change, this is not because of an unalloyed attachment to the past as such, but because of the irreplaceable value of what has been destroyed, its superiority to what has been substituted in its stead, which means its living strength and its efficacy. In other words – this is the conviction of the 'resisters' – the *ancien régime* and the Tridentine Mass realise, better than the *nouveau régime* or the *Novus Ordo Missæ*, what is the proper goal of every political or liturgical work. And yet, since a resistance is involved, this value of an immediate and living efficacy under the *ancien régime* is transformed into an ideal principle, continuing to enlighten us undoubtedly, but whose tranquil possession we have lost – a condition necessary for its inspiring power. How can we avoid the feeling that every effort at resistance and restoration will be deformed by historical reconstructions or will fall into what Pius XII, in *Mediator Dei*, called excessive archaeologism?

While it was being freely exercised, this inspiring principle, which one intends to safeguard, certainly did not manifest itself as such, in its naked essence. Immanent to political or liturgical forms, it animated them *invisibly*. But these forms were not immutable. Like everything temporal, they were subject to slow but continuous change, although not to ruptures or substantial alterations, just like a tree which grows and unremittingly becomes, from a tiny seed germinating in the darkness of the earth, a vast canopy of branches in the windy heights of the sky. The tree of history is in essence only the original principle itself in its incarnation. Undoubtedly the dislodging and revolutionary forces, by cutting down the tree of history, oblige resisters to distinguish it from the principle incarnated within it: the corpse proves the soul by its absence. Only after the French Revolution did monarchy become a theory and a doctrine. Before that it was something lived daily in the present; afterwards it is still lived, but almost always as an abstraction. And precisely for this reason, to obviate the constantly threatened risk of seeing the inspiring principle's reality transformed, under the new regime, into a conceptual cadaver, one is more and more strongly tempted to identify this principle with one of the concrete forms it assumes; some insisting on the last state – considered to be canonical – of its slow evolution, others, to the contrary, choosing to return to the supposed poverty of its primal forms. Is the true monarchy that of Louis XIV or St Louis; the true eucharistic liturgy that of 1962, St Ambrose or St Hippolytus?

Such is the general situation imposed by the revolutionary forces on the resistance. This is normally untenable and, because it is normally untenable, to remain steadfast demands abnormal behaviour. It is then that one becomes a royalist or even an ultra-royalist, a traditionalist or even a fundamentalist. But is one a royalist under royalty, a traditionalist under the regimen of tradition?

And so, often unbeknownst to those succumbing to it, spirit becomes identified with resistance. This nearly unavoidable perversion happens at the very moment when confidence in the forces of resistance overwhelms confidence in the spirit animating it. Here we pass from spiritual resistance to fortress-resistance. A kind of practical attitude emerges, an attitude which relies on what is most sure, on the reinforcement of human precautions to safeguard the essential. Discipline and the sanctions guaranteeing it are reinforced; with a continually heightened awareness of omissions and deviations, surveillance and denunciations arise. Orthodoxy is defined by a more and more geometric and formal rectitude of such a nature that deviations, previously infinitesimal and almost indiscernible, now take on the look of major heresies. Also, undoubtedly, a certain taste for the corporeal, inherent to the human condition, takes its toll; but above all we should see in this an anxious desire to assure the *efficacy* of resistance. Now, as seen in our

Spirit and Resistance

meditation on the term's etymological significance, resistance involves the occupying of a place, a cultural place obviously, the very one in which the forms of the spirit have taken shape. This is why the resisters proceed to fortify that place which they intend to continue occupying. They isolate it from the rest of the world, sealing up all of its cracks and outlets; nothing must penetrate, nothing escape. In this way they think that the spirit will be well guarded. However, this protective network is never enough, the enclosure never altogether hermetically sealed, hence the need for indefinite reinforcement. All too clearly the goal of this undertaking is more and more lost from sight, and replaced by an accumulation of means judged indispensable to its attainment. Spirit is wholly converted into resistance, down to the moment when one sees – too late! – that the very reasons for building such a high and powerful fortress have disappeared.

2. *The resistance of form*

It is important, then, to ask about the true essence of what is left, of what resists all change and outlasts every destruction. This is why we must let the natural order itself teach us, so as to find out what it says about the resistance of the spirit; but not losing sight, for all that, of the fact that what is valid for the natural order cannot be valid as such for the cultural order, to which spiritual resistance pertains.

When considering a living being, whether plant, animal or man, we are spontaneously inclined to identify its ontological consistency, the durability of its being, with that of its body, i.e. with the consistency of an organised material. With the vertebrates, for example, we have established a kind of hierarchy between the truly hard parts, chiefly the skeleton, and the softer ones, first the flesh (muscles and fatty tissue), next the liquids, like blood and lymph, and finally the much more subtle fluids, such as the nervous flux. As for the soul or spirit, when one agrees (in the case of a human being) to recognise its presence, one will tend to imagine something akin to the nervous flux, but even more subtle and, ultimately, having a much more fragile reality, something much less consistent and hard than bone and muscle. A massive and solidly framed body – that is true resistance; like a fortress it surrounds and protects the flickering flame of the spirit.

This spontaneous view is entirely false. To be convinced of this, and in default of a demonstration which I am unable to give just now, it is enough to observe that what is defeated and dies is the body, while the spirit, or what there is of the spiritual in the body, seems to enjoy a kind of perpetuity. Let us leave aside even the question of the immortality of the human soul, and consider only what there is of the spiritual in the corporeal. By this we wish, quite simply, to designate what Aristotle called a 'form', in so far as this form is an act, an energy, giving a form to matter. If this notion is viewed in its greatest simplicity, it will be seen to connote two basic qualities: *meaning* and *life*. Form is not, in fact, a spatial configuration, except under one of its modes; but it is what is meaningful in a physical being, which is to say what is intelligible and therefore what enables us to distinguish it from other beings. This is its structure, the organisation of its material, the totality of all the interconnections of a being's constituent elements, which can be grasped by the intelligence. This form is 'meaning' to the extent that it is *one*, for the unity of a multiplicity can only be the unity of a meaning, can only be semantic in nature – as is exemplified in language, where a multitude of signs are essentially 'one' and immanent to one another thanks to the meaning which unifies them. In the same way the different wheels of a watch are spatially distinct, but semantically within each other through the unity of the rational principle ordering them, or, one could say: in the unity of a *logos*. And this semantic principle is not a pure abstraction, not an entity of reason, although only the intellect may be able to grasp it, and even though it may never fall under the senses. It is a perfectly objective living and acting reality, a structure surely, but first of all and in truth a structuring activity. All too often we regard structure as an inert architecture, a mechanical assemblage which happens to animate, from without in some manner, a principle of movement, a soul or a spirit. Such a conception stems from a residual and hard-to-dispel Cartesianism. The animal-machine theory, the source of atheist materialism as well as spiritualist idealism, is surely the worst component of Descartes' philosophy. But, in reality, a living being has nothing of the hard, the solid, the resistant which might initially present itself as simply an isolatable and fixed bodily structure, a structure which would afterwards happen to set in motion an invisible vital principle. We tend to favour this false view because we take things in reverse order; we start with a cadaver bereft of life and study it as if it were identical to a living body, whereas, in the words of Bossuet, it is something which has no name in any language. A cadaver is not a body minus something invisible and non-corporeal, it is a *quite different reality* which immediately decomposes. From a strict biological point of view, there is no identity between the one and the other. If a bodily structure resists, does not become undone, this is because it is activity, energy, exchange, tension. At the very moment when this structuring and form-giving dynamism ceases, the consistency and resistance of the body also ceases and is undone: all the apparent hardness and consistency of bodily matter is only an appearance of subsistence. True subsistence is the form and, for the living, it is the soul.

Nevertheless, this is what the most constant experience confirms when considering, not just a being actually present in its individual singularity, but the permanence of forms in the duration of the universe. Such and such a pine, such and such an oak – which is to say such and such a quantity of individualised matter – becomes corrupt, decomposes and disappears; but the essence of the oak or pine, withstanding time, remains almost indestructible. Thus what form realises in space (in the deepest meaning of the term 'realise', since this is what *makes real*, what gives being to matter) is also realised in time, well beyond the length of an individual being's life, since the same form crosses the millennia and sometimes even geological eras. Without doubt it would be appropriate to add a few distinctions here and there. The working-out of a form relative to the present existence of a single living being is obviously not the same as that which assures the formal permanence of this type of being across the millennia. The first is realised through an informing of suitable matter, it stems from the physical in the Aristotelian sense, it is 'in act'. The second corresponds to the permanence of a possibility; in a certain way it controls the space–time reality of the physical world, and is not to be envisaged directly in its own form-giving operation, but in itself: it stems from the metaphysical order. And yet, however it may be with these differences, differences secondary to our subject, it is important to observe that a natural being's consistency, and therefore its resistance to destructive agents, is not assured by the solidity of the material apparatus which enables it to exist, by its opacity or physical impenetrability, but by its form, whether viewed in itself as a trans-temporal possibility or in the presentness of its form-giving operation. Besides, where is the unity and individuality of a being reduced to its purely material reality, when viewed on the sub-atomic level? Far from being impenetrable and opaque, such a being would present itself (an impossibility) as a more or less dense haze criss-crossed by a multitude of particle tracks. Now, as Leibniz says, a being which is not *a* being is not a *being* either. And this requisite unity can only be that of an intelligible form.

In point of fact, we cannot experience form 'in itself', as if it were a distinct material reality which would be interjected into and isolated from matter at the same time. We experience it only negatively, as that which, in matter, specifically resists destruction. Conversely, neither do we experience matter as such: this would be pure and simple non-existence. We grasp only dialectical states of tension of a single reality, both form and matter inseparably. Matter, in this reality, is everything which tends to defeat and degrade itself, while form is what opposes and retards this degradation.

Considered thus, matter obviously no longer designates, as with the materialists, the corporeal consistency of things. It signifies the cosmic usury which marks all natural beings, that is to say the totality of conditionings, and therefore the limitations to which their existence is subjected. In other words, no natural being can exist simply as an essence or a form. The existential actualisation of this being is subject to really distinct conditions (space is not time) and therefore really countable ones, both limiting and dividing. A pure form is a pure unity. All is one within it. Not being made from anything, it cannot be destroyed. But it exists as such only in the divine understanding. Its actualisation in our world implies its fragmentation, its articulation, its composition: a plurality of elements ordered one to another, an organised body. This is the only possible translation, given the multiplicity of existential conditions, of a form's intrinsic unity. Matter is therefore every existential conditioning which necessarily involves an indefinite divisibility, a vanishing close to nothingness at its extreme limit. If this divisibility, this crumbling, this pulverisation were ever to reach its end, at a single stroke corporeal reality would be worn away and annihilated. But, to put it concisely, what resists this permanent threat of annihilation is always the *form*, form which is resistance as such, or, one might even say, the differential, ungraspable in itself, which ultimately but completely distinguishes informed matter from nothingness.

3. *The resistance of spirit*

Such is, I think, what the philosophy of nature teaches us. But this teaching cannot be applied directly to the philosophy of *culture*, from which the art of spiritual resistance stems, and this for an obvious reason: the union of form and matter, or again, the informing of matter by form, is effected spontaneously, according to objective laws which define the very order of nature and structure it ontologically. Form is really and immediately immanent to matter, in such a way that the form-giving operations are carried out by virtue of the essence or nature of the being under consideration: it is enough for beings, i.e. natural beings, simply to exist for the form-giving process to be realised, for this is the process by which they have assumed an actual existence. In the order of nature, to exist is to be realised, and to be realised is to exist: it is precisely this which describes the world of becoming, for, in order to be, things have to become.

Things proceed differently in the cultural order, an order in which we are no longer dealing with individual beings or natural realities (both existing through themselves), but with being-signs constituting a world of representations. The matter–form pair can be used only by analogy: since matter is the aggregate of limiting conditions by which alone a form may be realised in the physical world, its cultural analogue will designate the aggregate of conditions by which an idea, a theme or an intention – in short a spiritual being – will enter into the world of culture or come to consciousness and, in a general way, be made manifest to men. This involves what is called 'forms of expression'. The pair matter–form thus becomes the pair form–spirit.

On the other hand, the relationship of spirit to those forms which manifest it culturally is not immanent and spontaneous, as in the case of natural beings: one and the same spirit, one and the same idea can be manifested according to different forms, forms which may therefore be of unequal expressive value, and this possibility is essential to the cultural order. This is because the human will, which freely chooses which forms to manifest, interjects itself between a spiritual theme and its modes of expression. Now to *choose* is to seek for the best, or for what appears to be such. Thus no spiritual reality automatically determines the forms of its historical realisation. Obviously we should not exclude exceptional cases in which the spiritual theme itself fosters its own forms for manifesting; poets and artists call this inspiration: the form seems to impose itself as self-evident. These cases are rare. Neither can we omit the case of the divine institution of religious rites; if we are believers, we have to admit that God himself chooses those forms which incarnate the spiritual essence of the rite. And, if he chooses them, or, at least, if he raises them up by the power of the Holy Spirit, this is obviously not in terms of an unthinkable arbitrariness, but in terms of the aptness of sensible elements for expressing invisible realities, which implies the existence of objective laws of sacred symbolism.

And yet neither of these two cases invalidates our description or renders the intervention of free will and intellect useless in mediating between the spirit and the forms of its manifestation. In the case of art, which brings us back analogically to the giving of form to a discrete individual being, the artist can always reject the form which seems to impose itself, and should even be suspicious of the deceptive faculties of the imagination. In the case of the divine institution of sacred rites (which brings us back to the permanence of the possibilities and archetypes prevailing over time), the religious person can always reject the forms which these rites have assumed, while, if he accepts them, as right reason bids him do, this acceptance is itself free and voluntary. It is even more so when this acceptance is maintained unchanged over time and takes the name of tradition. This is what I shall now examine.

Spirit and Resistance

Tradition is the perpetuation of what was in the beginning. Now it is normal and legitimate to think that at the beginning the Holy Spirit was not absent at the institution of religious rites in their sensible forms, even when this institution is human, since these forms, being the first, are destined to direct all religious history in a definitive way. Deviations are always possible, but are rightly secondary, each deviation presupposing a *via* (a way) from which it deviates.

Thus, corrcctly understood, the idea of tradition offers, as we shall see, a solution to the paradox of resistance expressed at the beginning of our reflections: as much as possible, it enables us to avoid the snare of fortress-resistance and to gain access to a true spirituality of resistance.

To become better aware of this, let us temporarily take the viewpoint of the adversaries of tradition. From this perspective, tradition appears to be a *counterfeiting* of nature by culture. Just like habit – tradition being merely its social or collective mode – tradition passes for second nature. It represents the immemorial duration of institutions and rites, political and religious custom, devotion and beliefs; everything that, almost unchanged, has crossed the centuries and which, to the eyes of the revolutionaries, continues to control our behaviour and lives. Perpetuated in this way, the social order seems eternal: nothing is more unshakeable than a tradition; it possesses the changelessness of a mountain, and, like it, will crush men and block the horizon to their future. To overcome it a tremendous effort must be exerted. But look! – the wrecking crew has only just begun when the whole building collapses.

In reality, no tradition stands and endures by itself. Tradition has no other strength than that of our fidelity; it exists and lives only by our existence and our life. We only have to cease giving it form by practising it and – instantaneously – it will return to nothingness. It expects everything from us, it is entirely at our mercy. In the same way Bernanos, in his *Dialogue of the Carmelites*, has the Mother Superior say: 'Remember, my daughter, that it is not the rule which keeps us, it is we who keep the rule.'

And, in fact, what is true of the relationship of spirit to the forms which manifest it in the establishing of cultural works is likewise true for their duration over time: the free will required for the one is also required for the other, and is then called perseverance and fidelity, which are simply other names for love and generosity.

For tradition expects us to give ourselves to it. Wholly impotent to constrain us (outside of recourse to the power of the secular arm, which always ends up weakening it), it hopes only in the innate nobility of people who are able to give themselves to what surpasses them, able to suspend the appeal of the immediate and the useful, able to become servants of the invisible and transcendent. But, by a miracle which is repeated throughout history, it is precisely at the very moment when we enter into the service of the transcendent that we are invested with our true dignity. It is in giving ourselves to what surpasses us and draws us upwards that we truly learn how to stand upright. For more than two centuries now, revolutionaries of every persuasion have been intent on freeing human beings from what they call oppressive and alienating traditions, so that we may stand with head erect beneath an empty sky. But, in so doing, they do not realise that they are depriving us of precisely everything, in the religious or political sphere, which keeps us from being discouraged after finding ourselves to be just one more thing among other things, one more nature among other natures. St Augustine says it admirably: we need to *fall upwards*. But how do you fall upwards if there is no force to lift you? In the sphere of moral and spiritual realities, what makes us stand upright is not some intrinsic and decisive rigidity of our nature upon which we could in some way lean, or which we only need to let blossom spontaneously in order to realise our verticality. This would be to forget that the spiritual order is that of the free will and that a will can only be moved towards an end which it seeks to attain. This end, being situated outside and above our natural state, lets subsist between itself and this state an empty space to be filled in with our freedom, and it is this space which gives us an opportunity to rise above ourselves. Only nobility obliges. Spiritual verticality is never 'acquired', we are never its possessors. It is always a *gift*, a grace which the norm, the Principle, grants to one who has become its willing servant.

To round off the Bernanos thesis we need to add that, exactly to the same extent that we keep the rule, the rule will keep us, but the one should not be confused with the other: that *the rule keeps us* is pure grace, pure miracle, an unmerited reward, whose transforming operation escapes our conscious sight; that *we keep the rule* is up to our good will, to our determination to remain faithful to what ennobles us. And this is the secret of true spiritual resistance, a secret which guarantees it against corruption. One committed to this way should know that nothing is owed to him. As firm and heroic as upholding it may be, we must never forget that it remains completely useless to the intrinsic power of the spirit. Of itself, our fidelity is already a reward; the rest does not concern us. We do not own the spirit whose guardians and defenders we have become. To keep watch over the treasure of sacred forms and preserve them in the face of indifference and widespread hatred is in itself honour enough to brighten a human life.

Besides, for one who has once understood the matrix function and the structuring power of the spiritual forms – the languages and the rites that tradition has delivered and confided to our generosity – it could not be otherwise. Well he knows that they are forms which build up humanity and perpetually save it from an ever-threatened decline, and that they likewise provide the radiance of the spirit with a means of expression not all that unworthy of its glory. Because they are sacred, that is to say 'set aside', because they deliberately break with the profane forms of daily life, they introduce into the tissue of human existence this saving distance, the only place where human freedom can breathe, the only situation in which it finds itself surpassed. And it is here, in this uprooting, in this suddenly yawning void, that the Spirit can pour the living waters of its grace and diffuse the fire of its light. Confronted with these truths which impose themselves on his mind, the man of tradition cannot do otherwise than enlist in their service, and commit himself to an unfailing spiritual resistance. But he will keep himself from ever forgetting – and this is the unique secret of an authentic spirituality of resistance – that a guardian is not a jailer, and that the fortress of tradition should not be a prison for the spirit. As well stocked with weapons and with determination as the sentinel watching from the highest tower might be, he leaves open, in the extreme weakness of his heart, that place where the God who sleeps in the midst of tempests will awaken.

Chapter 6

The Sense of the Sacred

The concluding remarks of the previous chapter lead us to finally shed some light on the *sine qua non* for a restoration of the sense of the supernatural, which is also the primary condition for its education and growth. We have seen how it died and what its gradual disappearance meant for the faith; we must now recall how it lives and forms itself. The sense of the supernatural is the sense of a higher nature, the capacity to have a presentiment of a reality surpassing the natural order, or that the possibilities of existence do not limit themselves to what we ordinarily experience (the real as spontaneously perceived and lived, or as scientifically construed). In order for this sense to be awakened in us, we need to have in this world of ours an experience of forms which, by themselves, refer to nothing of the mundane. This experience is given us by liturgical forms, that is, by symbols through which the invisible transcendent, the divine, renders itself more present. The totality of these symbolic elements (words, vestments, colours, music, gestures, places, temporal cycles, architectural forms, etc.) is what we call the *sacred*. Elements borrowed from the physical or human worlds are always involved – otherwise no experience of it would be possible – but they are set aside, separated from the natural order to which they originally belonged and to which they refer, and consecrated in order to render present realities of another order. The realm of the sacred is therefore a mediator between the natural order and the supernatural order.

However, sacred forms are not mediatory by themselves. Being signs, they realise their mediatory function only if they are 'full of grace', that is, only if they serve as a mode of expression for the ritual activity by which the first mediation, that of the divine activity of Christ, is rendered present among us. Thus we can distinguish three kinds of mediations. The first is that of Christ in his redemptive Incarnation: this proceeds from the supernatural to the natural ('And no man hath ascended into heaven, but he that descended from heaven', Jn. 3:13); the second is that of ritual action, the actual performance of a rite which is mysteriously identified with the divine action; the third is the mediation of those sacred forms which the ritual action signifies and without which it cannot be accomplished. This third mediation proceeds from the natural to the supernatural, while ritual activity realises something like a mediating fusion of the one with the other (the priest at the altar acts *in persona Christi*), a fusion which only an act and not an element of the world can realise. By this the redemptive sacrifice of Good Friday, the first and unique mediation accomplished once for all, is rendered present, in a sacramental mode and in the sacrificial liturgy of the Mass, to people in every age; or rather they themselves are rendered present to it, here and now, in its permanent actuality, through the mediation of those adequate forms which signify it in their eyes.

Sacred forms are, as we have just seen, tertiary mediations, with our need for them dependent on ritual activity, which is itself dependent on the divine activity of the crucified Mediator. Hence the modern mind's conviction that their nature is unimportant, that one can change them as one sees fit or even suppress them as much as possible, so as to avoid the risks of superstition, idolatry and liturgical formalism. Furthermore, each of these mediations can in their turn be the object of a challenge. The most Modernist of 'theologies' will cast doubt on the sacrifice of the Mediator, denouncing the inadmissible haggling of a God athirst for vengeance and his pardoning of the Adamic offence only at the price of his Son's blood. Lutheranism will reject the mediation of a ritual activity united to the sacrifice of the Mediator, denouncing this blasphemy which claims to add to the infinite merits of Christ on the Cross the supposed merits of a simple human liturgical action. Finally, a post-Conciliar and overly irenic Catholicism, desirous of giving pledges, if not to the first, at least to the second, will repudiate the sacred forms in the name of the rite's independence with respect to its means of expression, and will strive to attenuate what, in the liturgy of the Mass, too clearly expresses the sacrificial reality of the action accomplished.

We are not saying that the reform imposed since 1970 is to be reduced to the two motives just indicated. This reform had other, more remote reasons, some of which were rooted in a very serious and often scholarly desire for a return to the original spirit of the liturgy, which medieval piety had somewhat altered, while other reasons – the most dangerous – stem from a naively pastoral will to facilitate to the utmost the participation of the faithful.

What was the result? The spectacular thinning-out of practising members and the rapid, almost total disappearance, in a short time, of the clergy (at least in France) are surely not due simply to the liturgical reform. But one cannot deny that this is a powerful contributor, especially to the extent that, as we said at the beginning, the sacred forms of the liturgy are the first and most effective educators of the sense of the supernatural, without which the grace of faith cannot penetrate the human earth. Now the 1970 reform has had at least one incontestable effect, whether sought for or unexpected: the suppression of *liturgical rituality* as such.

A rite teaches two things. First and directly, by its very nature, its symbolic content, it declares a fixed theological truth, which the accompanying words (or doctrinal commentary) render explicit and make understandable. Second, in so far as it is a fixed, immutable, timeless and visibly extraordinary form, unusual for the profane world, hieratic and mysterious, it implicitly yet concretely teaches what a rite is: an ensemble of forms from this world, forms invested and regulated by a secret order in which something of the transcendent is rendered present. Now by changing the rites, we might well hope that the substituted rite more clearly expresses what the former rite expressed (this is sometimes the case); but what is unquestionably being taught is that the ritual order itself does not exist, since it is permissible to violate it, and so a new rite is no more a ritual than an old one. The revolutionary thinks that he is setting up a good institution in place of the bad one which he destroys: most frequently he is teaching the decrepitude of institutions as such, and the pleasure to be had in destroying them. Whether it be political or liturgical, revolution chiefly teaches revolution.

Such is the undertaking in which the reformers have been engaged with an unbelievable lack of awareness, at least in the case of the best-intentioned among them. They should have known that every true rite, beyond the particular teaching delivered through its own content, is telling us silently: 'I am immutable like eternity, I come down from the beginning itself and I anticipate the end of time, I am permanent like the order of God in which I have established you. While the millennia flow by and the ages change, I remain. Ever in me is your present; in me your ephemeral life can rediscover its surest meaning, because ever in me is the fidelity and the patience of Divine Love and its promise. You who are worn out by the whirl of time and things, you who have been torn to pieces, divided further and lost; come and see, I will gather you together again, unify you, calm you, for I am always the same; I am the language with which your fathers and mothers prayed, the words they pronounced, the song they sang, the deeds they accomplished; I am the long and still fresh memory of people when they remember God.'

But the substitute rite, louder than the advantages that it might possibly offer, proclaims: 'I am for today, tomorrow we will see. See how superior I am to the rite which I have replaced: better, more worthy of you, I am in conformity with the aspirations of the present humanity, I respond at last to truly Christian needs, much more authentic needs than those of the past: Catholics were superstitious then, passive, sheeplike, formalist hypocrites, pharisaical; today they are sincere, evangelical, pared down and fraternal. Rejoice and congratulate yourselves: the Church of the past is dead, and dead with it that Latin which you would not understand, those unseen gestures in front of the altar accomplished by a priest who turns his back on you. And besides, why should you not change me? An adult humanity is a free humanity. Improvise! Stop repeating. Express yourself, express your truth, your sensibility, the faith that is yours, be creative: your own wealth is worth more than a magisterium that always lags behind you. Burst forth! Celebrate!'

Certainly I exaggerate somewhat, but not much. This is why there is no room for astonishment if, of all the rites, the rite described in the *Novus Ordo* is the least followed,[1] since it seems that for many it is only a 'pretext rite' intended to shoot back the bolt of rituality and to open definitively the era of permanent revolution in the liturgy.

By evoking the immutability of the old rite, I am not unaware that I am neglecting the various changes this rite has undergone in the course of its history. This is an argument often used – and by knowledgeable liturgists – to prove to the partisans of the Roman rite that they are idealising the past and that, in reality, this immutability is only a myth. But this argument proves exactly the opposite. Although the *ritus romanus*, which in its essentials dates back to the fourth century,[2] might have undergone a number of changes (still, as for the ordinary of the Mass, it has remained unchanged since the end of the fifth century), all the while staying substantially itself, this is because, in good logic, its own consistency was of a foolproof solidity (otherwise it could not have been the *subject* of these changes), and because, on the other hand, these changes involved only *secondary* elements of the rite. To the contrary, the liturgical reform of Paul VI dealt with the essentials, it totally recast the rite (with the preservation of some secondary elements): a revolution decided by those in authority without precedent in the history of Christianity.[3] Which means that it should never have happened.

To impose so radical a change on a liturgical practice maintained for fifteen hundred years and more by the Roman Church is not only a blunder, it is also an error, without doubt one of the more serious ones committed by the magisterium in

---

[1] The *Novus Ordo* includes, not only the four Eucharistic Prayers, but also every regulation concerning it (rubrics, etc.). For example, to say the *Orate fratres*, the *Institution generalis* (§107) directs that the priest return to mid-altar and *turn toward the people*, which supposes that, previous to this prayer, he had turned *away from them*, as was done in the traditional rite. As promulgated, the *Novus Ordo* has been strictly applied almost nowhere.

[2] If not even to the apostolic age, as the popes, before Paul VI, have always affirmed.

[3] Cf. Mgr Klaus Gamber, *The Reform of the Roman Liturgy: Its Problems and Background* (Harrison, NY: Una Voce Press and the Foundation for Catholic Reform, 1993), chap. 4. The author concludes that the Pope did not have the right to impose such a reform.

the twentieth century. Surely certain rubrics needed to be simplified, certain incoherencies or ambiguities, certain disputable practices or practices of doubtful antiquity eliminated. There was a vast amount of work to be done, but done with the utmost circumspection and while keeping in mind these lines from Montesquieu, lines which ought to be meditated upon ceaselessly by every reformer: 'One feels the old abuses and sees their correction, but one also sees the abuses of the correction itself. One lets an ill remain if one fears something worse; one lets a good remain if one is in doubt about a better.'[4] What was needed above all was to restore the sense of the sacred, the sense of the liturgy, the mysterious celebration of the mystery of worship by the sacerdotal community of the priests and the faithful gathered together in the presence of God and his holy angels. Instead of this there was a complete upheaval, a cleansing by the void, and at the outset the suppression of the old Latin, the mother tongue of the Roman liturgy, the *universal*, that is to say the *Catholic* tongue, the hieratic and noble language, the necessary safeguard for the dignity of the rite.[5] The Church was deluded about its power. Inattentive to the harshness of the modern world, the clergy lived in a false security, like the beneficiaries of too rich a heritage who, once having squandered the treasure they thought inexhaustible, are surprised to find themselves bankrupt.

The question then does not have to do with the validity of the new rite, which should not be seriously contested (although those masses may be invalid where the celebrant does not intend to do as the Church wishes, that is where the sacrificial reality of liturgical action is rejected).[6] The question has to do with those sacred forms thanks to which the transcendent mystery

---

[4] *The Spirit of the Laws*, ed. and trans. A. M. Cohler, B. C. Miller and H. S. Stone (Cambridge: Cambridge University Press, 1989), p. xliv.

[5] Not to mention the destruction of the liturgical year, which amounts to a veritable 'profaning' of the temporal.

[6] Let us recall that it is not enough to admit the real presence of Christ under the species of the Eucharistic Bread for the Mass to be valid: Luther admitted a certain mode of Christ's presence *in* the bread and wine. Besides this we need to believe that the liturgical action accomplished is a real and true sacrifice, in its essence identical (not in its mode, which is unbloody) to the sacrifice of Calvary; which many so-called Catholic priests and theologians deny today.

accomplished on the altar is rendered present to our fleshly being, to our senses, to our heart, to our spirit. It is through these forms that we are given form and shape sacrally, through them the *Mysterium liturgicum* is communicated to us, through them it can shine forth on the world and vivify with its grace the entire body of the Church. In a few churches, a few monasteries, there are liturgies where the new rite is celebrated in Latin with undeniable dignity and beauty. But in general, and even where one cannot deplore any infidelity to the prescriptions of the *Novus Ordo*, where the congregations are fervent and prayerful, the decline in quality of the liturgical level, with respect to its rituality and sacral beauty, is striking. Certainly the masses of yesteryear were not always radiant or models of liturgical sense. Let us go further: since halfway through the Middle Ages the sense of sacred liturgy has been problematic in the West, whereas the Christian East has known how to keep it intact and powerful. Nevertheless, even in these deficient and sometimes conventional or mechanical celebrations, the quality inherent to the Roman rite preserved the essential and communicated an incomparable sense of the supernatural and the divine to the human soul.

It is this which has disappeared, it is this which should be rediscovered, under one form or another, with the help of God.

Part II

THE CONTEMPLATED TRUTH OF FAITH:
THE BODY OF CHRIST

Chapter 7

The Essence and Forms of the 'Body of Christ'

Philosophy teaches that the activity of our spirit is always determined by its object: it is the thing seen which reveals to the eye its ability to see, and the thing heard which reveals to the ear its ability to hear. It is the same for the sense of the supernatural. Only the revelation of the 'mysteries of the Kingdom' in the person of Christ can awaken it to itself and give access to the truth of its essence. This is why it is now appropriate to contemplate this icon of the Kingdom, which is none other than the *Corpus Christi* envisaged in its fullest and loftiest significance, this Body of Christ in eternal exposition before the Father, this Body where, in glory, the wounds of his Passion form a sign of the Cross.

'For Christ has entered, not into a sanctuary made with hands, a copy of the true one, but into heaven itself, now to appear in the presence of God on our behalf' (Heb. 9:24). 'He did not wish to efface his wounds in heaven, so as to show to his Father the price of our deliverance' (St Ambrose, *In Lucam* 24:39). 'It is fitting that Christ's body was resurrected with its scars so that he may present eternally to his Father, in the prayers that he addresses to him for us, what death he suffered for men' (St Thomas, *Summa Theologiae* IIIa, 54, 4).

The theme of Christ presenting the glorious wounds of his Passion to his Father in eternity dates back to the epistle to the Hebrews and has been constantly reiterated in Christian theology, as well as in the piety of the saints and the faithful. Now this theme contains a profound truth which I would like to expand upon briefly. Moreover, the seemingly 'sentimental' nature of this tradition invites us to seek out its metaphysical roots. In the passage just quoted from the *Summa*, St Thomas himself sets forth the following objection: 'The Body of Christ is resurrected in its integrity. But the openings of the wounds are contrary to the integrity of the body itself since they interfere with the continuity of the tissue.' As we shall see, it is precisely this objection which leads to the central mystery of the *Corpus passum*.[1]

However, before proceeding further, let us recall those principles which govern every meditative reflection on Christian matters. These principles are two in number: in Christianity, everything pertaining to its essence must be referred to the Trinity, while everything pertaining to its existence must be referred to the Incarnation. By 'existence' I understand the providential and legitimate forms which Christianity has assumed in the course of its history, and thanks to which it is rendered present to mankind. By 'essence' I understand the qualitative content of all its constituent elements, or, at another level, the archetypal reality of the Christian revelation as a whole. As to 'reference', by this I understand that the Incarnation and the Trinity are the models of intelligibility, or that they constitute the major speculative keys which respectively cast a living and more than adequate light upon both the existential forms and the essential truths of Christianity.

1. *The triple Body of Christ*

If the Incarnation is a major key to unlocking the mystery of Christian existence, this is because the doctrine of the Body of Christ – the element specific to the Incarnation – plays a central role. In fact, just as it is possible to bring all Christian metaphysics (the 'theological' point of view) back to the Trinity, so also it is possible to bring all 'physical' aspects (the 'economy' of the faith) back to the Body of Christ. This may seem surprising, for all too often we like to consider doctrinal truths *in abstracto* and, without being aware of it, instinctively suppress whatever seems foreign to the abstract nature of sacred doctrine.

However, we have but to glance through the New Testament to discover the high regard in which it holds the Body of Christ. I will cite only two groups of texts – well-known ones at that – but they must be reread with care in order to gauge the precise

---

[1] That is, the 'Suffering Body'.

The Essence and Forms of the 'Body of Christ'

importance that the *Corpus Christi* holds in Christian revelation: (1) the sixth chapter of the Gospel of St John (the discourse on the Bread of Life), and (2) the first epistle to the Corinthians, along with the epistle to the Ephesians, where St Paul establishes the theology of what will later be called the Mystical Body.

To these scriptural references I will add the second and less well-known theological doctrine of the 'Triple Body of Christ', about which a few words will be said. This doctrine is sometimes called the doctrine of the *triforme Corpus Christi* or 'Threefold Body of Christ'. The formula as such originates with Amalaire of Metz, Bishop of Trier and friend of Charlemagne,[2] but the sense in which we use it is that of St Paschasius Radbertus, abbot of Corbie.[3] It is with him that we find this doctrine most aptly formulated, and it will be reiterated in this way throughout the Middle Ages. St Paschasius and Godescalc, who quotes him some years later (attributing the text, and hence its authority, to St Augustine), speak of the *triplex modus corporis*[4] or the 'triple mode of the Body of Christ', because, as Godescalc notes in his *Liber de corpore et sanguini Domini* (831), Scripture uses the phrase *Corpus Christi* in three different senses. The New Testament uses the phrase (1) in the sense that 'the Church of Christ is his body: it is of this body that Christ is called the head and that the elect are called members'; (2) in the sense of 'the true flesh of Christ which is consecrated every day by the Holy Spirit for the life of the world'; and again (3) 'this body which is born of the Virgin Mary, into which the [Eucharistic] body has been transformed ... and which, now become pontiff, intercedes each day for us in eternity'.[5]

St Paschasius was by no means the inventor of this doctrine, for we find the following commentary by St Ambrose on a passage in Luke (17:37) – 'where the body is, there the eagles will be gathered together': 'We have no doubt as to what is meant by body, especially if we remember that Joseph of Arimathea received the Body from Pilate ... But the Body is

---

[2] *Liber officialis* (813) III, 35; *PL* 105, 1154–5.
[3] Cf. H. de Lubac, *Corpus mysticum* (Paris: Aubier, 1959), pp. 39, 299, etc.
[4] Cf. Lubac, *Corpus mysticum*, p. 338.
[5] *PL* 30, 1284–6; cf. Lubac, *Corpus mysticum*, p. 40.

also the subject of this saying: my flesh is real food indeed . . . and this Body is also that of the Church.'[6] Lastly we will quote a text by Honorius of Autun, who summarises the entire teaching:

> The Body of Christ is said to be of a triple kind: first, it is the Body incarnate of a Virgin, offered for us upon the altar of the Cross, raised to heaven after having conquered death, seated on the right hand of God; second, they call the Body of the Lord the promise given to the Church and which the sacerdotal power mysteriously realises from the bread and wine consecrated by the Holy Spirit. And thirdly the Body of Christ is the entire Church in which the elect are united like members of a single body.... The third Body is connected to the first through the second, so much so that one does not affirm that there are three Bodies as such, but only one Body co-ordinated by the Holy Spirit, just as in the human being the soul provides life to all the parts of the body.[7]

I shall shortly return to the last remark of Honorius. For the present I would like to consider further the doctrine of the 'Threefold Body of Christ' in order to develop its contents in full, something which to the best of my knowledge has never been done.

In fact, according to the Gospels, the 'Body born of the Virgin', which I shall call the *Corpus natum*, is itself presented under three different aspects. First there is the Body as it came forth from the womb of the Virgin Mary and which the crowds of Palestine knew as the vehicle of his human presence (I call this the *Corpus intactum* or *integrum* because it still existed in the perfection of its nature). Next there is the same Body which suffered the Passion and which is marked with the stigmata on account of our sins (this I call the *Corpus passum* or the suffering Body, the Body affected by the imperfections of our nature). And finally there is Christ's risen Body, the spiritual Body, and yet a true Body, because it is the true and permanent essence of the Body, as the Transfiguration clearly demonstrates (this I call the *Corpus gloriosum*, for the true perfection of the human body is only realised under the illumination of grace). Now it is

---

[6] *In Lucam* 17:37; *PL* 15, 1781–2.
[7] *Eucharistion* 1; *PL* 172, 1250. I have kept the name traditionally given to the author. But *Augustodunensis* seems to mean 'of Ratisbon' and not 'of Autun'.

The Essence and Forms of the 'Body of Christ'

a wondrous thing that this triplicity of aspects is also to be found in the 'Body of the Church' or *Corpus mysticum*. For does not the Church Militant on earth correspond to the *Corpus intactum*, does not the Church Suffering correspond to the *Corpus passum*, and is not the Church Triumphant in heaven typified by the radiance and splendour of the *Corpus gloriosum*? As for the *Corpus eucharisticum* (or sacramental Body), it is the operative bond of unity between the *Corpus natum* and the *Corpus mysticum*, because it renders the *Corpus natum* present to the intimate being of all Christians who receive Communion, and, by making their union real, builds up the *Corpus mysticum*, to which it is essentially ordered. Such are but introductory considerations, for this doctrine is so rich that one could continue to develop it indefinitely. And is there not also a remarkable congruence between the three modes of the *Corpus Christi* and the Three Persons of the Blessed Trinity: the *Corpus natum* being related to the Father, the *Corpus eucharisticum* to the Son, and the *Corpus mysticum* to the Holy Spirit? Within the extremes of each mode, might we not even establish similar analogical relationships, thus relating the *Corpus intactum* and the Church Militant to the Father, the *Corpus passum* and the Church Suffering to the Son, and the *Corpus gloriosum* and the Church Triumphant to the Holy Spirit?

Such a schema clearly shows that, in a certain way, the function which the *Corpus eucharisticum* performs between the *Corpus natum* and the *Corpus mysticum* may likewise be assumed between each of the extreme modes of the *Corpus passum* and, in a more indirect way, the Church Suffering (provided that we do not identify the latter solely with purgatory, but rather include in it that 'purgatory on earth' which is suffering lived in a Christian manner). This similarity of function shows the close relationship which more especially unites the *Corpus eucharisticum* to the *Corpus passum* (confirmed by the sacrificial nature of the eucharistic Bread and hence liturgical activity), as well as the relationship which unites the consecrated Host to the Church Suffering (confirmed by the union, like a living Host, of Christians in the unique sacrifice of Christ).

The following diagram summarises these considerations in graphic form:

FATHER
Corpus natum

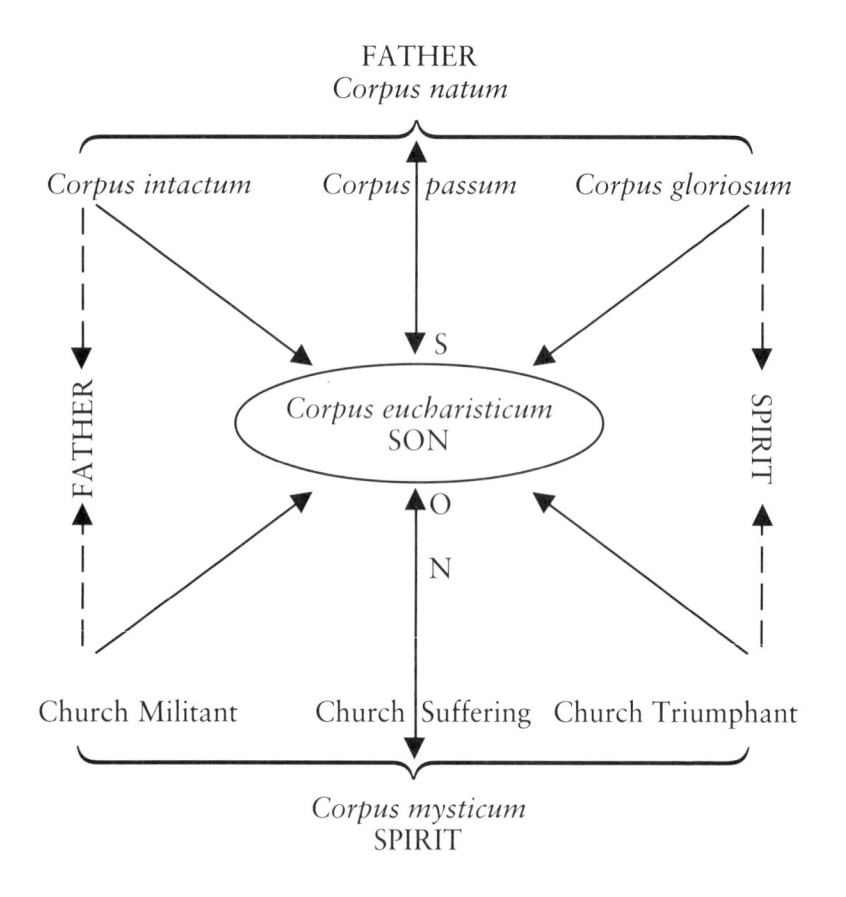

Corpus intactum — *Corpus passum* — *Corpus gloriosum*

FATHER · *Corpus eucharisticum* SON · SPIRIT

Church Militant — Church Suffering — Church Triumphant

Corpus mysticum
SPIRIT

2. Its unique essence

Now I return to the comment of Honorius of Autun regarding the unity of the Body of Christ, a remark also encountered in Paschasius Radbertus and in virtually all the other treatises dealing with this subject. The doctrine of the 'Threefold Body of Christ' is more than just a recognition of what Scripture tells us; it also carries with it certain doctrinal consequences: it affirms that these three are forms and modes of *one and the same Body*, and this is of great importance. We are often inclined to think of the *Corpus Christi* simply as the *Corpus natum*, or historical Body, and to see the other two modes as being no more than symbolic or metaphorical aspects of this. But if the doctrine of

The Essence and Forms of the 'Body of Christ'

the Threefold Body of Christ is true, then our usual manner of envisioning it is both coarse and inexact. In its proper and supernatural reality, the *Corpus Christi* is not to be identified with any of these three modes exclusively, for each one possesses an equal right to be called the *Corpus Christi*. Whether the Eucharistic Body or the Mystical Body, they are no less the Body of Christ than the *Corpus natum*, but are rather this Body in another manner. It follows then that, in its celestial principle, the *Corpus Christi* is a totally transcendent reality, far surpassing our usual concepts and imaginings.

Perhaps some will think that such speculation risks losing contact with earthly and historical realities. However, at the risk of offending those committed to concrete patterns of thought and who view the abrogating of the spiritual dimension as a matter of common sense and realism, it should be obvious that the Body of the First-born among the living and the dead could never be an ordinary body. Certainly for us, and from the only point of view in which we can situate ourselves at present, the *Corpus Christi* is above all the Body born of the Virgin, the Body which suffered the Passion and was resurrected in paschal glory. Certainly the Word was truly clothed in a flesh which was just like ours in all things, except for sin. But is this all there is to it? Are we to believe that the union of this Body to the hypostasis of the eternal Word differs in no way from our own? What are we to think of the Transfiguration – openly doubted by agnostic exegetes? If we reread St Paul we will come to a better understanding of what the *Corpus Christi* is, and perhaps we will begin to have some appreciation of what its Ascension means. If this Body can pass beyond the whole of visible creation and 'leave it behind', it necessarily follows that in a certain way his Body contains all of creation within itself. Some will consider this metaphysical stuff and nonsense! But why do such people not see that our ordinary way of looking at the world and history is false, illusory, abstract and unrealistic; that *reality* is not and cannot be a vanishing succession of perpetually ephemeral moments, an absurd and inconceivable dance of blind electrons? Can they not see that the marvellous events of the Incarnation and the Resurrection are specifically meant to revolutionise our way of seeing things, to induce us to enter a new order of Reality by aligning us with it and it alone?

The irruption of the Resurrection within our world tears us away – in proportion to our faith – from the horizontal relationships which connect us to each other and to things, that is to the ensemble of relationships which define the 'world'. It reorients us to the vertical relationship which springs from the Glorious Body ascending into heaven: a Body infinitely more *real* than anything we have experienced, a real and not a metaphorical Body which reveals, beyond the utmost reaches of our imagination, 'a new heaven and a new earth'; in short, a new creation which is in reality the true creation that was created *in Principio* – in the Principle. What is no longer understood by modern scriptural exegetes is precisely this: a change in the way we see and *know* – a *metanoia* – is demanded. Basically they are materialists (without knowing it, which is indeed the height of metaphysical infirmity), incapable of imagining the existence of a *corporeal* reality other than the fallen body of our daily experience.

Let no one accuse me of destroying the unique fact of the Incarnation which, as is rightly said, divides history in half. For I will ask: in what does this uniqueness lie? Certainly not just in its being a 'discrete timebound event', something 'here and now', for *all* historical events share in this; the smallest gesture, the least word of the most insignificant person, a pebble rolling into a ditch, all are discrete timebound events. History – the concern for history so dear to our supposedly 'down to earth' contemporaries – is *by itself* incapable of assuring the uniqueness of the fact of the Incarnation. This uniqueness pertains to its intrinsic and essential reality, the 'descent' of the divine into the human, which is also and more profoundly the 'assumption' of the human into the divine. In other words, a positive and qualitative uniqueness is involved here, not the negative and rightly quantitative uniqueness attained by mere historicity.

To summarise then, we need to acknowledge the archetypal reality of the Body of Christ, for it is in Christ that God has chosen us 'before the foundation of the world' (Eph. 1:4), and it is 'within him we have been created' (Eph. 2:10), within this Jesus Christ, 'image of the invisible God . . . *for in him all things were created* in heaven and on earth, visible and invisible' (Col. 1:15–16). Now this archetypal reality is the unique principle of all the forms assumed by the *Corpus Christi*.

The Essence and Forms of the 'Body of Christ'

Far from annihilating any of these forms, above all that of the *Corpus natum*, all of these forms subsist, to the contrary, within this principial Body in a permanent state, and it is by virtue of the unity of this principial Body that Mary, true Mother of the *Corpus natum*, is also true Mother of his Mystical Body which is the Church. And so we see that all the mysteries of the Christian religion are admirably verified and harmonised, since, in its perfect form, this religion is identified with the principial Body of Christ. What is the perfect Religion if not the work of salvation – the eternal accomplishing of the divine Will in the world? And what is this eternal accomplishment if not the whole of creation as God conceived it and wished it to be within his divine Intellect, for 'the glory of God is the salvation of the world'?

Chapter 8

The 'Body of Christ' and the Work of Salvation

1. *The work of creation and the work of salvation*

The work of salvation, as theology instructs us, is greater than the work of creation. Nevertheless there is a certain similarity between them which is realised in the *Corpus Christi*. In fact, as we have shown, the principial Body can be considered the prototype of all created forms (the First-born of all creatures), for, being the Body of Christ, it is the most perfect of all forms. However, we must not forget that in philosophy the word 'form' does not designate the bodily enclosure of a being, but rather its essence. It is in this sense that we see the divine Word as the 'source' of prototypical forms, the eternal synthesis of 'possibilities'. There is of course a close relationship between the essence-form and the corporeal form, for the latter is an image and spatial expression of the former. This is why the principial Body, the corporeal form (in an analogical sense) of the divine World, can be seen as the prototype of all created corporeal forms, and hence of all creation. (In the same way it could be said that, through his human soul, Christ is the prototype of all created spirits and therefore of invisible creation as well.) Between the *Corpus Christi* and the created world there is, then, a direct relationship. And yet this relationship is no less ontological for being exemplarist in nature, which is to say, for being the model for an image. It is not for nothing that the being of man is made in the image of God. Although I will return to this shortly, for now we can already see how this provides a certain intelligibility to the mystery of the redemptive Incarnation, and therefore to the *opus salutis* realised by the *Corpus Christi*.

First of all, if there is a need for salvation, there must be a circumstance which demands it, a state of loss. And if there is a state of loss, this is because there is something *able to be lost*, something which has actually been lost. In other words, the original state of justice and holiness was not purely and simply natural to man. Adam was not an unconscious robot. The theomorphic nature with which God had endowed him should have been actually realised, actively and freely directed to God. In default of this, the human state of being 'an image of God' is obscured and deeply wounded. This is a law which holds true for all creation, whether visible or invisible, paradisal or fallen, namely that *nature must be realised*, must *become* what it *is*. The difference between the Adamic and post-Adamic state is that the supernatural grace needed for this realisation was given to Adam *at the same instant* that his nature was, while it is conferred on fallen man only through baptism, which is to say only though sacramental participation in the death of the *Mediator*. Even though this sacramental grace was conferred on Adam at the moment of his creation, it was able to be lost, for it required the free assent of the recipient and therefore could be refused.

What is lost by this refusal is the grace given immediately to nature. As a result, *nature is reduced to a destitute state, a state of nakedness*. Nature is despoiled: 'they saw that they were naked', says Genesis of our first parents after the Fall. But this state of nature laid bare is not our 'natural' state. Far from interpreting this as a reduction of Adamic being to its 'pure nature', as do certain theologians, we should see instead a state of wounded nature, of a denatured nature, because, reduced to himself, man is less than a man: 'Original sin is something other than a mere withdrawal of grace leaving nature completely "intact" and restoring man, so to speak, to his normal state.'[1] Man is in fact precisely that being who, in order to be what he is (the image of God), must want to become such (realise the likeness). What is true, in the thesis of a reduction to a purely natural state, is that man *sees himself* as reduced to this (they *saw* that they were naked), sees himself as a being who, having been withdrawn from grace, having been cut off from the divine sphere of influence, has conquered his autonomy and abstractly

[1] Henri de Lubac, *Surnaturel: Etudes historiques* (Paris: Aubier, 1946), p. 101.

The 'Body of Christ' and the Work of Salvation

thinks of himself as a pure generic essence. Conversely, when the order of grace offers a revelation of itself to us, it seems to be outside of the natural order, it seems 'naked' and foreign to everything which pertains to the human estate. Corresponding to the naturalist and abstract idea that fallen and 'withdrawn' man has of himself is his supernaturalist idea of divine assistance. What is true in this view of an extrinsic grace which remains foreign to the natural order is that, since original sin consisted in this very will to separate nature from grace, a remedy can only come from an initiative of the divine Will. Or again, since original sin consisted in this very will to separate nature from grace, the remedy can only be a *willingness* to reunite nature with grace: to give nature back to the grace that has been removed from it, so that grace can once more accomplish its work within it. This divine Will, which asks again for a human nature in which to accomplish its work, is grace itself, or, even better, the uncreated Source of all grace. As such, this uncreated Grace transcends the whole of nature and is identical to the saving Will of the Father, with the Incarnation of the Son in Jesus Christ being the achievement of its plan. As I have made clear, in this theandric operation divine grace is no longer received within human nature as it was for Adam, but, conversely, it is human nature which has been received within the grace of the Word descended among us. Humanity has been 'assumed', lifted up by the descending grace of God, for 'no man hath ascended into heaven, but he that descended from heaven.' At that moment the eternal vow of the Lord of the worlds to seek a created receptacle in which to confide the work of his mercy was accomplished.

And yet God could not have obtained this created receptacle that is the humanity of Jesus Christ had not Mary given her consent. Now Mary, preserved from original sin, is the pure creature as God had willed it to be and just as it came forth from his hands. In her we contemplate human nature in all its purity. But what is this pure nature? The angel of the Annunciation reveals it: it is 'full of grace'. In her, God has found the perfect creature whose will makes itself the receptacle of the divine Will ('I am the handmaid of the Lord') to make possible our salvation ('be it unto me according to thy word'). Here we clearly see how the work of creation and the work of salvation, the *opus creationis* and the *opus salutis*, are reunited; it is in Mary that this joining, this reversal, this conversion of the creative work into the redemptive work comes about. It is she who offers Grace that human nature needed for its work, she who gives to the divine Word a human nature perfectly obedient to the Father's Will, which calls for the incarnation of the Son. And it is therefore within Mary that the key to the supernatural mystery of our nature abides. If, by a prodigious miracle, God, in his creative act, has consented to the existence of something other than himself and granted it being, then by an even more prodigious miracle, he has made *himself* a creature through his Incarnation. In the *opus creationis* all things existing outside of God were ordained to contemplate him. Once this ordination had been ruptured, there was 'nothing left to do' but for God personally to enter this cosmic exteriority so as to lead it back to himself, so as to turn it back towards his face. St Paul calls this going out, this exodus, this 'extinction' or humiliation of God *kenosis*: 'Jesus Christ, who being in the form of God, did not consider his equality with God a possession to be jealously guarded, but emptied himself [*ēkēnōsen*], taking the form of a servant' (Phil. 2:5–7). But this going out is done with a view to a re-entry; this exodus has in view a return; this extinction has in view an exaltation; this *kenosis* has in view a *metanoia*. As Jesus says in St Luke (5:32): 'I come . . . to call sinners to *metanoia*', to a return to being, knowledge and love.

Thus, according to a formula reiterated by a number of the Church Fathers, 'God has become man so that man might become God.' And just as the humanity of God is the work of his grace, so also this divinisation of man is the work of Christ's grace. Man does not become God by nature, 'which is even more foolish than heretical' (Fourth Lateran Council, Denzinger 433), but by participation in the divine filiation of Jesus Christ. And because the act of the redemptive Incarnation is truly accomplished by the kenotic descent of the eternal Word into a human body, the work of salvation is effected by an act of extreme and consummate humiliation in this same Body. This Body is a body of grace; it is grace embodied, the corporeal source of all grace and sanctification. The ultimate result of this divine descent is that it points out and defines the way back to eternal Love and blessed Unity. Like lightning flashing out from the supreme Mercy, this Body traverses all the degrees of universal existence until it reaches the ultimate limit, the lowest and least degree of reality, with which it invests itself as with a garment.

Having done this, and because it could not lose its identity with the principial Body, this *Corpus natum* of Christ, through which the *opus salutis* is accomplished, appears as both the centre of and the model for all creation, as the *paradigmatic synthesis* of the universe. Is not the *Corpus natum* composed of those very same elements which make up the universe? Is not matter, both inert and living, to be found within it? Except for this notable difference: ordinarily these elements possess only a natural existence, but, in the *Corpus natum*, by virtue of the grace of the hypostatic union, by the union of the two natures, divine and human, in the unique hypostasis of the Word, these elements are joined to a divine substance. And this is why the *Corpus natum* must be the lordly centre of the entire cosmos, and why everything accomplished within this Body, by virtue of its centrality and lordship, is also mysteriously accomplished within the world. 'For in him all the fulness [*plērōma*] of God was pleased to dwell, and through him to reconcile to himself all things, whether on earth or in heaven, making peace by the blood of his cross' (Col. 1:19–20). By its divine virtue the *Corpus natum*, the paradigmatic synthesis of the universe, becomes a sacramental synthesis. Having been placed on the Cross, the *Corpus natum* casts its salvific shadow over the entire earth, effecting a kind of cosmic redemption. 'The death of Jesus on the Cross', says St Thomas Aquinas, 'corresponds to the universal salvation of the entire world.'[2] And St Gregory of Nyssa observes (*De resurrectione Christi*, oration 1) that 'the form of the Cross, radiating out from the centre in four different directions, denotes the universal diffusion of the power and the providence of him who hung upon it.' And this is why one can speak, as does the French Dominican Gonet (1616–81), of a veritable divinisation of the universe. 'By the Incarnation', he says, 'not only human nature, but all the other creatures of the universe have been raised, in some way, to the divine grandeur

---

[2] *Summa Theologiae* IIIa, 46, 4.

and a divine existence. In an admirable way, the entire world has been ennobled and embellished and, as it were, divinised.'[3]

Perhaps we can now begin to grasp why the relationship which unites the *opus creationis* with the *opus salutis* passes through the Body of Christ. In point of fact, it is only because this Body is eternally and principially the paradigmatic synthesis of the universe that it can be its sacramental and redemptive synthesis. And this also explains why the *Corpus natum* represents the Christian religion, for it is only the 'form' by means of which the *opus salutis* continues through the centuries. But not only is the *opus salutis* more admirable than the *opus creationis* in its 'mode' (in as much as God consents to make himself creature), it is also such with regard to its end. For the state of the ransomed and Christified creature is greater than this creature's original state. The redemptive Incarnation does more than 'save the world' from the abysses opened up by original sin. Not only does it check the fall towards indefinite multiplicity, it also occasions the creature's entrance into Glory. It introduces us into the circumincession, into the reciprocity of the Three Persons of the Blessed Trinity, into that round of love which unites these divine Persons among themselves.

2. The mystery of the Blood poured forth

Now I shall attempt to penetrate in greater depth some of the more important aspects of what I have tried to investigate in a general manner. And so, little by little, we shall draw closer to the metaphysical significance of the eternal exposition of the *Corpus passum*. With this in mind I shall turn to the mystery of the Blood poured forth.

First I should point out that, while the mystery of the Body which I have been discussing refers primarily to the Incarnation, the shedding of the Blood refers more specifically to the Redemption. Certainly, one implies the other, and we should speak of a redemptive Incarnation as we do of only a single Eucharist. This unique Eucharist is, however, in conformity with the model established on Holy Thursday, consisting of two

---

[3] *Clypeus theologiae thomisticae* (Antwerp, 1700), vol. 4, disp. 3, no. 5, p. 349.

consecrations, and is realised through two transubstantiations of bread and wine. As for Good Friday, let us recall that the two events, the death of the Body and the shedding of the Blood from the open side, are clearly separate.

Thus it seems that we can distinguish between the 'effects' of the Incarnation and those of the Redemption. In the quotation of Father Gonet above, the divinisation of the world is effected as a function of the Incarnation alone; it is a consequence of the eternal Word assuming an earthly body. As a result of this all the corporeal elements are, at a single stroke, elevated to a glorious reality. By its very being the Body of Christ 'reveals' a truly supernatural mode of existence to the world and saves it. On the other hand, the Redemption is a result, not of the mere corporeal *being* of Christ, but of the *virtue* of the shedding of his Blood. Redemption corresponds then to an accomplished action, to a sacrifice effectively consummated, to the dolorous Passion in which this Body is delivered up. Thus the *kenosis* of his Incarnation, by which the divine Word is emptied of its divinity, is followed and completed by the *kenosis* of his humanity, in which he is emptied of the Blood of his corporeal life. In the mystery of the Blood poured forth, it is no longer the Body as paradigmatic synthesis of the universe which effects the divinisation of the world by being immersed in this world, but, on the contrary, it is the most inward life of this Body which streams down over Creation, immersing it in the Blood of the Lamb. The Body saves by its mere presence; the Blood ransoms by its sacrificial Act.

Here once again we find that law proper to the human world spoken of previously. Being has to be realised, it must become what it is. Only in this fulfilment is the efficacy of its virtue revealed. In the relative order it is as if the act, to the degree that it manifests what is hidden in being, is more important than being itself. Because the conditions of created existence impose a veil over that inner virtue which lies beneath a being's visible form, the unveiling of this virtue requires the rending and the death of this form. Only in annihilation does being disclose its virtue. Thus the Body contains the Blood as its proper mystery, its interiority, its strength, its life.

By the shedding of its Blood, the *Corpus Christi* is transformed from paradigmatic synthesis of the universe into sacramental synthesis. To the very extent that it is sacrificed, that is, separated from the world, set aside and given to God, it becomes the sacrament of the cosmos. As is well known, the sacred is defined first as a separation, and the 'etymological' connection – in the symbolic sense – between *sacrum* and *secretum*, the past participle of *secernere* (which means to separate or set aside), conceals a profound truth taught by Scripture in several places. The fourth chapter of Genesis informs us that the sacrifice of Abel was accepted by God because it realised the true essence of sacrifice, and this because Abel chose and *set aside* the first-born of his flock, and of these their fattest parts, for consecration to God. We learn the same in the Book of Exodus, where Moses had to take off (set aside) his sandals before entering the holy ground on which the Burning Bush was blazing. A portion of this world can only become a locus for the divine presence when its links with the rest of Creation – its horizontal relationships – have been broken and a link with the Creator – a vertical relationship – re-established. Thus it was that the smoke of Abel the Just's sacrifice rose vertically to heaven, while that of Cain's remained parallel to the earth. Since the act of creation is like a 'venturing' of God 'outside of himself', in so far as God, by creation, reveals himself to the outside world, to someone other than himself, to re-establish equilibrium and safeguard the very existence of the created, clearly, in a certain way, the world needs to 'venture forth' from itself and return to the Principle which gave it being.

With the sacrifice of the *Corpus Christi*, however, it is not just a portion of the world which returns to God, but, because of its mysterious identity with the cosmos, it is the whole world which is virtually reintegrated into its eternal Origin. And this is why the sacrifice is accomplished on the Cross, which unites the horizontal and the vertical. In this way the perfection of the sacrifice (*sacrum facere*) is realised and all creation is consecrated to the Uncreated. And in this same manner all previous forms of sacrifice are abolished, being contained supereminently in the sacrifice of Christ.

The Body of Christ, transfixed and 'lifted up' on the Cross, is separated from the earth and enters heaven, bearing witness to the fact that the world is not 'in the world', but in God. This perfect realisation is more than a 'separation', for, if such were the case, the sacrament of the Body would only be defined in negative terms. Although the negative aspect of the sacred is a separation, its positive interiority is the active presence of the divine. By means of this transfixed heart the world effects a reversal, a conversion (*metanoia*) of its own centrifugal course. To the *kenosis* of the Cross is added the *metanoia* of the saving Blood, which checks the expansion of the cosmos and leads it back to its immobile Centre. Just as in the existentiating act, it is the 'interior' of God that becomes exterior, or rather 'exteriority'; so also, in the saving act, it is the interior, or rather the 'interiority' of the *Corpus Christi*, that reveals itself externally, an interiority which, having been poured forth 'for many', leads cosmic exteriority back to divine interiority. Because it is the revelation of the mystery of celestial life springing from the very heart of God to lead all things back to it, this Blood which streams over the world effects a true cosmic baptism.

The same considerations apply, *mutatis mutandis*, to the sacrament of the Eucharist. The bread (or Body) corresponds to the perfection of being, while the wine (or Blood) corresponds to the perfection of life. This is why the words of consecration express, in the first case, a mystery of identity ('Hoc *est* enim corpus meum' – For this *is* my Body), whereas, in the second case, they express instead a mystery of redemption ('His est enim calix sanguinis mei, novi et æterni testamenti, mysterium fidei, qui *pro vobis et pro multis effundetur in remissionem peccatorum*' – For this is the cup of my Blood of the new and eternal testament, the mystery of faith, which *will be shed for you and for many for the remission of sins*). By itself the sacramental Body 'summarises' the cosmos; it is a portion of earthly bread, composed of the same elements as all earthly beings, but transubstantiated – 'transelemented' as some of the Fathers say – so that, in its turn, it is the entire earth which is transubstantiated within it. Conversely, by being poured forth over the world, the Blood saves by its action. The Body is the centre of space, towards which all things converge and in the substance of which Creation recognises a deifying transformation. The Blood is the centre itself poured forth and bestowed on all things, communicating its power of centrality to the universe, revealing that 'the centre is everywhere and the circumference nowhere.'

Also, the salvific working of the Blood is in a certain way superior to that of the Body. Or one can say that the Blood, relative to the Body, represents something more profoundly 'mystical'. The relatively 'exterior' mode of the Body contains the Blood which, like an inner mystery, is the whole deifying reality of the grace of Christ. But this offering of his inmost grace to 'the many' is surely one of the greater paradoxes of the Christian religion. The open side of the crucified Body through which gushes the effusion of water and blood is the 'folly of the Cross', the mystery of interiority poured forth and communicated to cosmic exteriority, so that it might recover the profound and transcendent dimension of its divine interiority. Only in the Blood of Christ is the grace of divine filiation perfectly established, our deification virtually realised. As a result, in baptism, which is immersion in the death and resurrection of Christ, it is a truly divine Blood which flows in our spiritual hearts, and which, in the words of St Peter, renders us *divinæ naturæ consortes*, 'partakers of the divine nature' (II Pet. 1:4). This is why St Paul declares: 'Do you not know that all of us who have been baptised into Christ Jesus were baptised into his death? We were buried therefore with him by baptism into death, so that, as Christ was raised from the dead by the glory of the Father, we too might walk in newness of life. For if we have become one in being with Christ through a death like his, we shall also be so through a resurrection like his' (Rom. 6:3–5).

Chapter 9

Metaphysics of the Eternal Exposition

The Body and Blood co-operate in the same restoration, the same return of the creature to its Principle. Through man, the central creature, the entire universe returns to God. The created world is renewed because it is baptised in the Blood of the Lamb, 'a lamb without blemish or spot ... destined before the foundation of the world' (I Pet. 1:19–20). This is a 'new creation' for, as St Paul tells us: 'Therefore, if anyone is in Christ, he is a new creation; the old has passed away, behold, the new has come' (II Cor. 5:17). And the Apocalypse speaks of 'a new heaven and a new earth; for the first heaven and the first earth had passed away, and the sea was no more' (21:1). In this vision it seems that the world itself partakes of the universal Body of Christ, partakes of that which is the glorious Pleroma, the *Corpus mysticum* whose model and operative sign here below is the Church.

Now, in eternally presenting the wounds of the *Corpus passum* to the Father, Christ is also presenting the *Corpus mysticum*, which incorporates the restored and renewed universe. All of this, then, is subjected to the Father's gaze under the figure of the Son's transfixed Body. But what is the significance of this exposition? Why does the glory of heaven not efface the marks of the Passion? Has not the former state of things disappeared? Has not everything become new? How is it possible for what has occurred in time, namely Christ's Passion, to leave traces in eternity? The answer to these questions involves, in a certain manner, the totality of Christian dogma.

First of all, if we can pose such questions, this is because the wounds of the *Corpus passum* exhibit imperfection, and it seems surprising for this imperfection to subsist in a state of perfect glory. Moreover, these wounds are the ransom paid for our redemption, a ransom required because of original sin. These wounds are then a proof of our sin, which is itself an occurrence within creation. In the restoration achieved by the redemptive act, should they not disappear along with our sin in such a way that the creature recovers its original perfection? But such is not the case, and it is perhaps here that the deeper meaning of the superiority of the *opus salutis* over the *opus creationis* is revealed.

Without doubt, and in agreement with the text of Genesis, creation is good, and this despite the fact that the work of the 'second day' – because it is a work of separation – cannot be qualified as such. But the good of creation is only relative, for only God is absolutely good: *Nemo bonus, nisi Deus solus*, 'None is good but God alone,' says Christ in St Luke (18:19). God alone is absolutely perfect, hence the perfection of the creature can only be relative. This means that it conceals within itself a possibility for imperfection, which is inseparable from the nature of the created and which is a kind of negative aspect of its finiteness. In the earthly Paradise this possible imperfection is prevented from becoming actual only to the extent that Adam, cultivating and tending the Garden, obeys God and actively realises the perfection of his theomorphic nature, without tasting of the fruit of the tree of the knowledge of good and evil, which symbolises, at the very centre of Paradise, the virtual imperfection of the created, or, if you like, the distance separating every creature from its uncreated Source. But this distance is not an estrangement if the creature stays close to God, submits itself to God's will, ontologically turns itself towards him, and somehow 'forgets' or 'ignores' this estrangement, being mindful only of the traces of divine splendour with which the Creator has touched all things and which it finds first in itself; it is mindful of them and contemplates them so as to adore, through them, its Creator.

Adam's theomorphism, from whence all of his nobility derives, can also, as we have seen, be the occasion for his disgrace. And the father of lies has 'employed' this very theomorphism to set a snare for the first man: 'in eating of the fruit of the tree of the knowledge of good and evil you will be *like God*,' says the serpent; as if promising them that they would know the *underside* of things. For Adam before his fall knew, in fact, only about Creation's 'theomorphic surface' – only about that face which Creation turns toward God and wherein God loves to be reflected. This created mirror of the Uncreated is the earthly Paradise. But, at the very instant that the act of disobedience is accomplished, the virtual imperfection concealed by the created condition is actualised and unfolds. The *state* of estrangement, or the distance of the created with respect to the Uncreated, becomes an *act* of estrangement and a fall.

Let us consider the vertical axis which unites the earthly Paradise at its centre to the creative Principle, which, in the biblical account, is described as the tree of life. This tree can be traversed in two directions: from below to above in a movement of obedience and adoration, or from above to below in a movement which turns away from God to possess the creature. The tree of the knowledge of good and evil is but the same vertical axis seen in its descending aspect of revolt and disobedience, and hence of the Fall. This is why it is said that this tree is also *at the centre* of Paradise. In so far as there cannot be two centres, the same axis of the world must be involved, but seen in reverse. The Fall is an act which effectively realises this inversion, Satan being not the image but the ape of God, his caricature. This inversion of direction, this satanic 'possibility' realised by man, is sometimes represented by a serpent coiled around the trunk of a tree, its successive loops symbolising the movement of a spiral descent. The identity of the two trees is signified by the image of Christ on a Cross surrounded with leaves, the upward prolongation of one and the same tree trunk. (One example of such a Crucifixion from the fifteenth century is painted on gilded wood and is preserved at the municipal museum of Pesaro, Italy.) Moreover, Christ was crucified between the good and the bad thieves: between good and evil. To corroborate my analysis let me point out that if, in Paradise, the tree of good and evil is, as it were, hidden within the tree of life, on Calvary the situation is reversed. The good and evil crosses encompass the life-giving one. The reason is that, to Adam's eyes, good and evil appeared in Paradise as a secret which God wished to reserve to himself, as something hidden 'inside' of things. Adam's sinful act exteriorised this false interiority which excited his covetousness and, at the same time, revealed its true nature. But, in its turn, Christ's redemptive act reveals, at the very centre of this exteriority, a new interiority, a mysterious heart, the very heart of the tree of life where the sap of divine grace has never ceased to flow: and this sap is the Blood of Christ.

However, to actualise the descending aspect of the world-axis necessarily prolongs the vertical towards the lower depths of Paradise, and hence reveals the dark and lower face on the underside of Creation. This overstepping of boundaries towards the lower regions is inevitable. When we consider the original configuration as a single perpendicular axis transecting a horizontal paradisal plane, clearly this paradisal plane *blocks* and in a certain way 'sends' the light of this ray back toward its divine source. This creative ray can 'actualise' a descending path only by passing through and beyond the horizontal reflecting plane, indicating an unstoppable plunge towards an empty and indeterminate 'lower point', symbolising in this way a vertiginous and indefinite plunge into the infernal abyss.

Original sin actualises the virtual imperfection of the created, kept from manifesting itself by Adam's contemplative obedience. More precisely, sin *is* this actualisation; it 'opens' the door to the underside of Paradise. It is the door itself, the door of inferior possibilities, the *janua inferni*, which is opposed to the door of heaven, the *janua cœli*. Mary is the 'anti-sinner', and this is why it was fitting that she be conceived immaculate.

But, for the created itself, this actualisation of negative or limiting potentialities is very far indeed from being a revelation of its own finiteness. If such were the case, sin would find its own end within itself. Quite the contrary: sin is utterly ignorant of its own nature; sin lives in – and lives by – the illusion of its indefinite power. The indefinite is the finite's potential for seeing itself as having an infinity of power. The paradisal plane 'closes' the cosmos. Sin gives the creature the illusion of opening up this space, of enlarging it and even making it limitless. Moreover, if the creature is to retain an awareness of this illusion, it has to be constantly reactivated, so that the Adamic race is condemned to perpetual transgression, to the repeated and interminable destruction of every trace of paradisal finiteness still left in the human state. For the indefinite is analytically inexhaustible.[1] The smallest segment of a straight line, however finite, is

---

[1] This remark by René Guénon, in his book on the principles of infinitesimal calculus, is a metaphysical key.

indefinitely divisible and will never be exhausted by such a division. And this is true for the totality of created things. Sin consists precisely in involving humanity in this analytical grasp of the created, by which it pretends to discover in finite beings this false infinity of the indefinite. Thus sin itself is analytically indefinite and inexhaustible; and, let us note in passing, this is one way of understanding the perpetuity of hell.

To 'escape' from this, then, we need to exhaust the finiteness of the created, synthetically and at a single blow, by passing instantaneously to the limit. Only the more *can do* less. Only the truly Infinite can exhaust the finiteness of the created and reveal to it its own limits and imperfection. Put in simpler terms, only God can save us. Despite the fact that this seems so obvious as to verge on banality, we spend our time wishing to save ourselves. Only the Infinite can make the finite truly *be*, that is, cause it to exist and reveal it in all its truth. This is precisely what the Incarnation and, in particular, the *Corpus passum* – the Body marked with the stigmata of the Cross, in other words marked with human finiteness – realise and accomplish.

In this Passion, where the Body of Christ is crucified upon the cross of the sinful contradictions of creatures and cosmic finiteness, the very truth of the created stands revealed. And this is why it becomes forever 'visible' in the Word's eternal exposition of his wounds to the Father. The state of the glorious Body is the state of the true Body; the *opus salutis* is greater than the *opus creationis* because it is the completed truth of this Body. Out of evil God has drawn a greater good, the greatest possible good. And this is why man, ransomed and saved in the glory of heaven, *can fall no longer*: it is because the finite, by the grace of the Word's Incarnation, has truly exhausted the lower dimension of its finiteness, it carries it within itself. Such a being can no longer fall because, for it, there is literally no longer any 'below'. Hence, far from it being necessary to ask why the Body of Christ, the supreme perfection of the creature, could be affected and stained forever by imperfection, we must understand that, on the contrary, it alone can be truly marked; and it is in this sense that St Paul declares: 'For our sake he [God] *made him to be sin*, so that in him we might become the righteousness of God' (II Cor. 5:21). The finite as such is ignorant of its own finiteness; the created as such is ignorant of its own original sin. To know its own being is, for the creature, to know its own nothingness. Thus, only the one who is knowledge incarnate can be made nothing, can be made sin. In realising the essence of sin in his own created existence, he exhausts and completes it in its very finiteness and manifests the 'justice' of God. And so, only the one whose body is perfect can manifest in that same body the truth (justice) of the created. Bearing the marks of its finiteness, the *Corpus passum* teaches us that God alone is 'good'.

This Body thus knows its own nothingness existentially; but, obviously, such a knowledge is simply bodily death and is only brought about in death. This is why the scars of the Passion of the divine-made-human can only appear in their definitive truth through the death of Christ. At the very moment that death is passed through and conquered, at the very moment when the Passover of our Christ is accomplished, these scars become no longer a passion submitted to 'from without', but a determination coming from his very being. The exteriority which could 'affect' the Body of Christ is internalised, inscribed as a permanent possibility upon its own glorious substance. Indeed, this Body becomes in some way 'untouchable' from without, and this is why, in St John (20:17), Jesus says to Mary Magdalene: 'Do not touch me.' It can only be reached from that divine interiority into which it has been reintegrated, a reintegration which will be manifested only at the Ascension. Hence the explanation given by Christ of the *noli me tangere*: 'For I am not yet ascended to my Father.' The way of love, symbolised by Mary Magdalene, can no longer humanly embrace the Body of its Beloved here below, however much its desire. The risen Christ is master of his 'tangibility' which, as we have said, subsists by virtue of a permanent possibility; it is he himself who presents himself to be seen and touched, so that his apostles may have faith and bear witness to what they have seen. This is why St John, a few lines after the encounter with Mary Magdalene, relates the episode of St Thomas, who is invited to place his hands in the 'openings' of the Lord's Body, openings which have become the doors through which his glorious humanity grants access to his divinity. Hence the extraordinary cry of St Thomas, who does not say: 'I have touched the living body of Jesus,' but rather: 'My Lord and my

God!' For God gave the risen Christ to be made manifest, 'not to all the people, but to us who were chosen by God as witnesses' (Acts 10:40–1).

This is why Christ brings the gloriously resurrected *Corpus passum* before his Father in the Ascension, for then the scars of his Passion take on a new meaning, or rather recover their most profound meaning, by a veritable transmutation of their cosmic significance. These scars, as we have said, are the marks of the inevitable finiteness of the created. But this finiteness of creation is also its salvation – provided however that this finiteness be actualised as such. These glorious scars, the holes in his hands, feet and side, *these holes are breaks in the integrity*[2] *of the created's finiteness* which bear witness to this finiteness – without which nothing could have marked this Body – but which, at the same time, realise the very end of this finiteness, completing it through its own negation and, as a consequence, ransoming it and saving it. Here, in these wounds, in this aperture into the heart of the world, the world ends, finiteness ends. Here the uncreated Infinite begins.

Such then is the metaphysical reason for the *Corpus passum* in the divine state, a reason which simply expresses what in the last analysis can be called the end of finiteness. But one final mystery remains to be explained, the one which we have referred to as 'the eternal exposition'; for Holy Scripture clearly states that Christ 'now *appears* in the *presence* of God on our behalf' (Heb. 9:24). My interpretation will be along the same lines, with the eternal exposition of the *Corpus passum* assuming its full meaning once we grasp the analogical connection between it and God's viewing of Creation at the origin of time as described in Genesis. In this cosmogonic vision, God casts his gaze in the direction of the world, and the goodness that he sees in the world is a reflection of his own, or even of his immanence therein. In the eternal exposition of the *Corpus passum*, the world itself is presented to the Father, offering itself to the Father's gaze as the transparent mirror of his transcendence,

---

[2] *Translator's note*: The French reads 'solutions de continuité', which alludes to the statement of St Thomas (S.T. IIIa, 454, a.4) quoted in Chapter 8. Standard English translations of this passage use 'solutions of continuity' and 'breaks in the integrity'. The latter version was selected for the sake of clarity.

for *nemo bonus, nisi Deus solus*. The cosmogonic vision of time beginning corresponds to the eternal exposition of time fulfilled. In presenting his transfixed Body to the Father, the Word is offering an icon of the universe, patterned after the truth of its finiteness, to the gaze of the monarchical Deity.

I say 'icon of the universe' because the *Corpus Christi* in fact recapitulates all creation, and because, just as this Body 'issued' from the bosom of God in the beginning, so also this Body has issued, without disruption, from the womb of the Blessed Virgin Mary. Now in both instances, it is the Holy Spirit who is at work. It was he who brooded over the primordial waters at the origin of the world; and it was he who covered Mary with his shadow on the day of the Incarnation. By his efficacious means the *Corpus natum* is brought into the world, and it is always he who is leading the finiteness of the created to its fulfilment, that is to say who leads the *Corpus intactum* to the Cross, even to death and transfixion. It is again he who leads all finiteness back to its infinite root by actualising, through the Church, the building up of the universal *Corpus mysticum*, which, by virtue of its identity with the *Corpus passum*, bears the same stigmata. It is then that the Father, the monarchical Deity – in response to the exposition offered to him by the Son's universal Body stigmatised in this way – can eternally pour forth, into the wounds in the hands and feet, and into the opening in the side, the divine Blood which is the Holy Spirit himself, so that all things may enter into the circumincession of the infinite Glory.

Chapter 10

The Prophetic and the Sacramental Functions of Scripture

> *Here is how you should understand the Scriptures: as the unique and perfect body of the Word.*[1]

1. Three or four Bodies?

We have contemplated the mystery of the *Corpus Christi* in its three forms as made known in Scripture and as elaborated doctrinally in the Middle Ages. But is not Scripture itself also the Body of Christ? Although not explicitly affirmed by any revealed text, Patristic tradition could not help but see the ensemble of the two Testaments in this way, as is seen in the citation from Origen quoted above. Should we then speak of a fourth Body of Christ?

To tell the truth, the relationship which the scriptural Body maintains with the *Corpus natum* differs somewhat from the one maintained between the Eucharistic Body and the Mystical or Ecclesial Body: this latter relationship only exists from the incarnation of Jesus Christ, which the two terms of the relationship prolong until the end of time and enlarge to the dimensions of humanity; while the scriptural Body 'precedes' the *corpus natum* by harking back to the very beginning of things, since it tells of the genesis of the world. It does not seem that Origen, who so forcefully stressed the relationship of the Eucharistic Body and the Word of God, ever spoke of the Incarnation in connection with the incorporation of the Word in Scripture. So why call Scripture the 'Body of the Word'?

This (life-giving) metaphor follows from the fact that the Son is characterised by St John as the *Logos* (or *Verbum* in Latin), that is to say the Word and, necessarily, the Word of God. This designation is created then *out of* an analogy, an analogy which

---

[1] Origen, *In Ieremiam*, PG 13, 544c.

presents the phenomenon of language: just as the human word utters the thought of a human speaker, so the divine Word utters the Thought of the divine speaker. But, temporally, we know of the Word of God only by Scripture. And, as there can be in reality only one sole Word of God, who is the Eternal Word, this temporal word (of God) is identified with this Word in its most profound sense. However, we would not know this temporal word without the language-related signs which it assumes: therefore we can consider these signs (the 'letter' of Scripture) as the body of the unique Word. We are indisputably within the scope of a comparison, whereas the *Corpus natum* stays within the scope of ontological unity (just like the Eucharistic Body); as to the Ecclesial Body, it is situated within the order of grace and glory. To summarise, one could say that if, by Scripture, the divine Word is made human word, it is made flesh by its incarnation in Jesus Christ. And only secondarily, with regard to the *Corpus natum*, can the scriptural word be called 'body'. As for the essence, there is then a closer relationship between the Eternal Word and the scriptural word – since both are 'word' – than between it and the *Corpus natum*, or, *a fortiori*, the *Corpus eucharisticum*; but as for existence, the relationship is the opposite: the Eucharistic Body communicates the very reality of the Body of Christ (and, by concomitance, his divinity) to our being, whereas the Body of Scripture communicates the reality of the Word chiefly to our intellects – both contributing, each in its way, to the building up of the Mystical Body of the Church.

Having made allowance for these various functions, we may continue to speak of the three forms of the *Corpus Christi*: a scriptural form, a eucharistic form and an ecclesial form, each one being a particular mode of the Body born of the Virgin: a mode of revelation (the Scriptures), a mode of presence (the Eucharist), and a mode of accomplishment and totalisation (the Church).

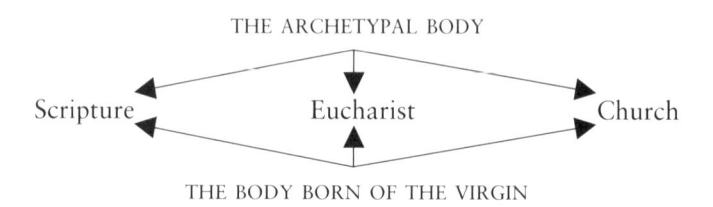

THE ARCHETYPAL BODY

Scripture ⇔ Eucharist ⇔ Church

THE BODY BORN OF THE VIRGIN

Thus set apart, the *Corpus natum* might be considered as the manifestation in time of the archetypal and eternal Body of Christ, 'the first-born of all creatures'.

That said, everyone will recognise that, apart from the liturgy, nowhere has the disappearance of the sense of the supernatural created more havoc than in the domain of Scripture. This is why we should now recall how God's Holy Word can be truly contemplated as the Body of Christ in the verbal icon of the Scriptures.

2. *The three co-ordinates of the real and the three phases of Sacred History*

Every living culture based upon a sacred Scripture is a perpetual rereading of that Scripture, in which the present is decipherable (readable) only in the light of the archetypal text where meaning has been spoken inexhaustibly and definitively (a 'rereading' is moreover one of the meanings of *religio*). Thus it is not only the Bible which is read by the Jewish or Christian people, it is also, and perhaps above all, the history of the Jews and the Christians which is read by the Bible, or, if a less blunt formula is preferred, which is decipherable through and thanks to Scripture. It is from Holy Scripture that this history, in each of its major events, receives its meaning and its truth. The rapport of a people or a religious world with their founding Book – which is called Tradition – is not then a one-way street. Without doubt the New Testament is open to the eyes of the faithful, is proclaimed in their ears so that they heed it most attentively. But the act of reading does not end with the text (with all due respect to many of the exegetes for whom the letter becomes practically an end in itself), even if it is first necessary to enquire into what is written. Neither do we think it ends with the Gospel mission (with all due respect to many of the pastors for whom the spread of the message alone absorbs all of religious life), even though we also need to communicate the Good News.[2] In truth, the Book read becomes in its turn the interpreter of human history: a light shines from it, its function is to illuminate the

---

[2] This is basically the principle of Karl Barth's exegesis: the proclamation as hermeneutic criterion.

real life of believers and to reveal the significance of the times, for want of which they remain indecipherable or, even worse, falsified and distorted in their profound truth. The Sacred Book is a mediator between God, who reveals himself there, and men; it is also a mediator between men and their history, which is prophetically announced and given its most authentic meaning in its pages. Just as the soul, according to Aristotle and St Thomas, gives form to the body, so Scripture 'gives form' to the historical body of the Church in its life both past and present; it directs it, structures it and actualises it so that, from one to the other, it creates a union which could be called substantial or ontological.

The first condition for such a 'form-giving' to be possible is that Scripture itself be seen as a primary, archetypal and founding event, the inaugural and basic reality of which should not be placed in doubt. In any case, whatever a thing's order may be, one generally speaks of its place, time and nature (or form, or quiddity): it is 'here', 'now', 'just so'. According to the world of common experience, these three determinations let us 'get a bearing' on its reality:[3] although their being applied to something individually does not make them fully real, except at the point of their convergence. However, in terms of points of view, a single one of these determinations might be preferred (without explicitly denying the other two). Physicists often, and materialists almost always, conceive of the real only under the category of space: what is 'there' is what exists. Thus they tend to neglect the categories of time and nature. On the other hand, historians and people generally, when they think about human life (theirs and that of others), perceive it instead as a temporal reality, a becoming, forgetting its spatial dimension and often (but with greater difficulty) its nature as well. However, the third determination, which is nevertheless 'essential', does not seem to enjoy a similar preference. To consider an event's form (its meaning) while neglecting its space–time setting passes easily for an idealist fault and is equivalent to denying its reality. No one reproaches the materialists or physicists for a lack of realism, although in fact classical mechanistic physics, which reduces

---

[3] Other determinations may be interjected (quantity, for example), but I leave them aside.

Prophetic and Sacramental Functions of Scripture

all bodies to stable geometric configurations, is quite simply false, the solidity of bodies being energetic in nature. In the same way, no one objects to the realism of the historians or common sense when memory (whether scientific or poetic) reduces living bodies to the temporal series of their acts (*res gestae*, things accomplished). Neither should there be a suspicion, then, of idealism with respect to a reading of the Scriptures which opts for the quidditative or 'semantic' dimension of a sacred event.

But three distinct orders of events are to be envisioned here, according to the three essential phases of Sacred History. From the origin to the fall of Adam, I will speak of a metahistorical phase; from the Fall to the tower of Babel, of a parahistorical phase; and lastly, starting with Abraham, of an historical phase. In the first phase we should not take our bearings on perfectly real events carried out with the help of their space–time co-ordinates, since the latter did not yet exist as such. Certainly, the creation of the universe and of man in his paradisal state unfolded according to certain existential conditions, which, in a more general way, can be seen as relationships of *coexistence* and *succession*. But these relationships assumed the forms of space and time properly speaking only with the exile from Eden. This is why we cannot imagine them: we need to designate them symbolically, aided by the analogical correspondence which the relationships of coexistence and succession maintain with the space and time of our experience. This in no way implies that events so designated are themselves pure symbols, or, as is said nowadays, simple poetic images. The reality of the designated does not depend on its mode of designation. In the parahistorical phase, we clearly find ourselves in the presence of our space–time world. But the configuration of this space and the rhythms of this duration are different from those we know, to such a degree that the account of events taking place, considering just their space–time determinations, can only be synthetic and approximate.

3. Semantic guidemarks for sacred events

No means are therefore left for expressly 'taking our bearings' and attaining to something of this pre-historical reality, other than its quidditative or semantic determination. And this is normal. If we represent the space–time co-ordinates by two orthogonal axes defining a horizontal plane (the spatial axis by the right angle in front, and the temporal axis by the right angle at the back),[4] the axis of quiddity will be represented by a vertical right angle, perpendicular to the space–time plane. This representation clearly shows that what we grasp of the semantic determination, on the space–time plane, is a point, the trace of the vertical, but which, in itself, is a determination that crosses other planes of existence. To be precise, when combined with space the semantic axis determines the bodily form, and when combined with time it determines life: the bodily covering is quiddity in space; the living individuality is quiddity in time.[5] Nevertheless, in itself, this semantic determination 'escapes' the limits of space–time conditioning and, hence, continues to denote a reality, even though the other two determinations can no longer be used *as such*.

[4] Space corresponds most directly to width, therefore to what is 'to the right and to the left' (this right–left orientation cannot be formulated abstractly, but is identifiable only with respect to the body of the human observer); time corresponds more directly to length: it is 'before' us and 'behind' us. Cf. my *La charité profanée* (Bouère: Editions Dominique Martin Morin, 1979), pp. 236–7.

[5] In our geometric representation, these two points are only one, which means that nothing is completely 'lifeless', nothing is totally inert. Absolute inertia is an asymptomatic extreme (nuclear physics speaks of the 'half-life' of a particle and shows us the energetic consistency of matter). But there is, obviously, a kind of antinomic polarity between pure form, realised in the geometry of the crystal, and pure life, realised in the melody of the psyche. From mineral spatiality to the temporality of the soul, nature sets before us all of the intermediate degrees, which by no means excludes relatively absolute discontinuities between the human, the animal, the vegetable and the mineral, for only the more can do the less: according to the natural order, the ladder of beings descends (a body without soul returns to the mineral state), it does not ascend (a molecule will never enter the vegetal state, a plant the animal state, an animal the human state; evolutionism in this sense is a physical and metaphysical impossibility). Without doubt, the advent of the plant may have been conditioned by a certain arrangement of the mineral state, and so forth, but this should not mean that this arrangement produces or engenders the plant (and so forth), which forms an organisation of a complexity qualitatively incommensurable to that of the mineral. These discontinuities can only be bridged from 'on high', which is to say by a divine creative act, necessary in each instance.

Prophetic and Sacramental Functions of Scripture

To tell the truth, far from being exceptional and obliging us to make an intense conceptualising effort, this case is on the contrary the object of a rather common experience. We are constantly experiencing realities which do not lie entirely within space–time, and yet they *exist* beyond the shadow of a doubt: there is a love within us (whether conjugal, filial or other) which orients our life and accompanies it, transcends the passing days, remaining identical to itself in its own specific being despite its variations and deepenings, without which we would question ourselves about this reality's mode of existence. This is not to be reduced, however, to a simple alteration of the soul (which would be an 'affective' idealism just as unsatisfactory as cognitive idealism). And what is the space–time *identity* of a nation, of an industrial firm, of the French Revolution, of the Roman Empire, or of the Académie française? Yet we speak of them as realities able to act and suffer, which have or have had certain marked effects in space–time, but which should not be identified with these traces and which continue to act even when these traces have vanished.

The mode under which we can attain to the metahistorical or parahistorical realities of Scripture is chiefly relative to their semantic dimension. This implies that they are to be seen above all as 'significations'.[6] As for historical realities, realities whose space–time conditioning is that of our present world and whose situation can be depicted, in terms of their quiddity only the contingency of their surroundings matters. Assuredly, in sacred history, everything is sacred, places and times especially, and everything has a meaning. But we have to organise things in hierarchies, since we cannot account for everything without getting lost in an indefinite analysis. Moreover, the circumstances themselves most often are only of interest through their symbolic significance. This is why the different categories of biblical narrative I have distinguished present us with events related chiefly according to their semantic determination. And this is also why these narratives and events not only have to be objectively studied and investigated in and for themselves, but

---

[6] I repeat that I am by no means reducing them only to significations ('ideas' in the psychological sense); but, since their substantial being cannot be attained in itself, we become aware of it essentially by means of its semantic modality.

above all serve as spiritual keys for completing and deciphering history as a whole, as well as the present life of God's people. To the very extent that they present themselves as having 'meaning', they enjoin us to make use of them as 'operative forms', having a form-giving power in the life of the children of Abraham. These 'operative forms' are, then, a bestowal of that holy form consigned to this life by the Lord's grace, as well as a deciphering of its destiny.

4. *The sacramental function of Scripture*

We are dealing with two distinct functions here, although in reality they are inseparable: the hermeneutic function of *deciphering*, which consists in reading Church history (but also the history of each of its members) in the light of the archetypal events[7] related by Scripture; and the active form-giving function which consists in *living* every moment of our existence in the founding light of these same events. The first function I will call prophetic, the second sacramental.

The prophetic function of Scripture by no means signifies merely the announcement by the Bible of the future unfolding of history, such that we would have to seek out the times to which such predictions might be applied. I do not completely dismiss such an interpretation, for it is only too obvious that the Holy Books do include announcements of this kind, and that some signs have been given therein. But we know neither the day nor the hour, and can only keep watch. Besides, if this was what I had in view, I would not be speaking of archetypal events. As for the events themselves, they may have an 'annunciatory' character, but their most basic importance lies elsewhere. If they are prophetic, it is because they constitute divine messages, definitive revelations; it is because they are 'oracles of the Lord', his spokesmen, communicating the idea that God 'makes himself' out of human existence and by this alone is our existence comprehensible *in its full truth*. In other words, in these archetypal events, the basic meaning of every

---

[7] These events are not contingent ones and do not partake of the fleeting moment, but are 'archetypes', founding and definitive acts, ever-present and ever-current models, permanent and life-giving norms: Christ's acts are *eternal*.

Prophetic and Sacramental Functions of Scripture

human life, individual or collective, and of every historical destiny, is announced and expressed.

But the sacramental function sets us on the path of an even more profound aspect of these archetypal events, which will make what I mean by this more understandable. And for me to speak of a sacramental function is not surprising; this is no misuse of language nor metaphor, but ecclesiastical tradition. Before the seven sacraments were definitively specified (about 1148 by Peter Lombard), numerous Church Fathers and illustrious Doctors had ranked Scripture among the 'sacraments'. True, the term had a much broader scope at that time than from the twelfth century on. It was in fact used to translate the Greek *mysterion*.[8] Thus St Augustine speaks of the *divinorum sacramentorum libri*,[9] that is, of the books of the divine sacraments (= mysteries), by which we must understand the teachings of Scripture hidden from unbelievers. But, from the fact that the Greek *mysterion*, and more often its plural *mysteria*, also designates sacred and ritual acts,[10] its Latin translation *sacramentum* benefits from the same semantic richness. Sacrament is not only the mystery of Christ's birth, death and resurrection, it is also the rite which communicates the grace of his redemptive Incarnation.

> There is a mystery [says St John Chrysostom], when we consider things that are other than those we see ... One is the judgement of the faithful, another is that of the infidel. I myself, I understand that Christ has been crucified and forthwith I admire his love for mankind; the infidel likewise understands and reckons this as folly ... Having become aware of baptism, the infidel thinks it only water; I myself, not considering simply what I see, I contemplate the purification of the soul effected by the Holy Spirit.[11]

A significant text: Scripture proclaimed and understood is no less a '*mysterium*' than the administering of baptism. Let us

---

[8] Which the Vulgate also renders by *mysterium*.

[9] *De utilitate credendi* 17, 35. The same formula is used by St Jerome, who speaks of the 'sacraments of the Scriptures', *In Isaiam* 1:6, PL 24, 207c.

[10] On account of its technical use in the vocabulary of the Greek mystery cults.

[11] *In I Cor.*, hom. 1, no. 7; *PG* 61, 55.

not see here a doctrinal confusion between the Sacraments, properly speaking (producers *ex opere operato* of the grace of *salvation*), and the sacramentals, or rites accompanying the Sacraments, the grace of which acts not only 'by the virtue proper to the work effected', but also 'through the virtue of the one effecting it' (minister of the rite and subject of the rite). To the contrary, there was never the least doubt in this respect in all of ecclesiastical tradition; it is baptism that confers the saving grace of the Blood of Christ on a human being, not the reading of the Bible or the recitation of the *Credo*. But the use of the terms *sacramentum* and *mysterium* contribute strongly to maintaining Holy Scripture within the sacral order, from which, I think, it should never have been separated; otherwise it becomes a text like any other. This is why the ritual proclamation of the Word of God during the sacrificial liturgy is necessary: not only for instructing the faithful, but also so that they know and understand that a sacred act is involved and not a profane reading. This is the proper place for the true *lectio divina*. There is nothing surprising if, in the ninth century, Paschasius Radbertus, the celebrated defender of the real presence in the Eucharist, 'lists as sacraments: Baptism, Confirmation, the Eucharist; next the Incarnation, the solemn oath, the whole redemptive work and lastly Holy Scripture.'[12]

5. *Mystery and archetype*

Ritual significance and scriptural significance are inseparable. 'Between the one and the other,' writes Cardinal de Lubac,[13] 'the interferences are so numerous and the relationships so profound that the two *Testamenta* have been unanimously seen by tradition as the workplace of all the *sacramenta*, the hiding-place of all the *mysteria*: "*duo sponsi ubera, ex quibus lac surgitur omnium sacramentorum*".'[14] Only in this light from

---

[12] Mgr Bartmann, *Précis de théologie dogmatique*, vol. 2, p. 232; 'oath' because such is the primary meaning of *sacramentum* in Latin.

[13] Henri de Lubac, *Corpus mysticum*, 2nd edn. (Paris: Aubier, 1949), p. 57.

[14] William of Saint-Thierry, *Expositio altera in Cantica*, PL 180, 488c: 'the two breasts of the bridegroom from which we suck the milk of all the sacraments'.

the *mysteria* do the realities spoken about in Scripture reveal their nature as archetypal events.[15] Here also tradition comes to confirm the conclusions of philosophical reflection. *Mysterium* has referred, in fact, since the early years of Christian thought, to *typos* (= 'type', which the Latin renders as *figura*, but in the sense of 'exemplary figure'). The word is recommended by a prestigious authority, since St Paul had used it in several places to characterise the nature of events and beings of the Old Testament with respect to the New, thus establishing Christian hermeneutics and defining the prophetic relationship which unites the first to the second.[15] Moreover, the original meaning of *typos* is 'mark' or 'imprint' (cf. typo-graphy). And sacred events and facts are indeed the 'marks' and 'imprints' left by the revelatory activity of God in human history. Now, just as with the seal of a king we see the wax impression of the form and not the seal itself, so with this divine activity we know the figure, the sensible imprint, but not the profound and spiritual reality, which can be marked only with the help of its *typos*.[16] This is why St Justin, combining *mysterion* and *typos*, teaches that 'the *mystery* of the lamb which God ordered you to sacrifice as the Passover was truly a *type* of Christ'.[17] Conversely, he calls 'mystery' what Tradition will call the 'typical sense', as when Isaiah announces the virginal birth of Christ.[18]

6. *Scripture and prayer*

When I speak of a sacramental function of Scripture, I am staying within the grand tradition of the Church and am not misusing language. Moreover, as I have stated, the term 'sacramental' is

---

[15] Adam is the *typos* of Christ (Rom. 5:14). The reality signified by the *typos* will therefore be the *antitypos*: thus baptism is the 'antitype' of that 'type' which is Noah's ark (I Pet. 3:21). But *antitypos* also assumes the sense of 'figure' and not reality (Heb. 9:24).

[16] The distinction between a sensible form and a theological content is expressed with the help of the *sacramentum–mysterium* pairing, whenever these terms are not synonymous: '*sacramentum* and *mysterium* differ in that *sacramentum* is a sign signifying something visible, whereas *mysterium* is something hidden signified by this visible thing' (Alger, *De sacramentis*, PL 180, 753).

[17] *Dialogue with Tryphon* 40.

[18] Ibid., 68, 6.

to be taken *lato sensus* here, and not in the specific sense of a rite of blessing or exorcism; this broad sense seems well founded to the extent that the list of the sacramentals should never be complete. In this respect the case of Scripture is analogous to that of prayer. Not every prayer is a rite, since it can assume the aspect of a freely formulated personal request or even pass beyond all form and language. But it becomes a rite when it consists of an act, and when this act is accomplished in conformity with an intrinsically sacred rule, canon or formula, which is to say by divine institution (direct or indirect). The virtue of ritual prayer (contemplative, prayer of adoration or intercession, public or private prayer) depends not only on the intention of the one praying, but on the sacredness of the form within which this intention is realised. Having come from God, this form really communicates a divine virtue for spiritual transformation, provided of course that the human subject is inwardly disposed to receive this grace. At this point a supernatural *habitus* is established in the soul, by which it is rendered more and more 'apt' for its divine destiny, whereas, lacking this inward disposition (a sign of our irreducible freedom), the sacred form cannot impart the virtue which is within it and is its *raison d'être*. One may repeat the holiest of formulas – recite the Our Father, invoke the Name of Jesus – but one is not praying, one is pronouncing 'in vain the Name of the Lord'.[19] For Jesus has said: 'It is not the one who says "Lord!

---

[19] Let us recall that this involves the *second* commandment, which therefore precedes all the others except for the recognition and adoration of God alone. This commandment should concern not only 'oaths' and the profane use of the Divine Name. Prohibition of profane use is the sign of a much more lofty reality, that very reality which the *second* verse of the Our Father designates: *sanctificetur nomen tuum*. To hallow the Name (as one keeps holy the Lord's day) is precisely to render this Name 'holy'. And since it is already so in itself, this means to 'render it holy' within us and for us. In other words, the act of naming – which is its effective utterance – should be a sanctifying act and not a simple pronunciation. And this act will be sanctifying to the extent that the form of the Name (its language-related structure, obviously, but also its essential significance – for the Name should be in the heart and not only on the lips) truly informs the soul with that which it utters, and therefore to the extent that this soul, as a docile material, will let the Holy Spirit effect the work of the Name within itself, as Mary, on the day of the Annunciation, let the divine *Pneuma* effect the Incarnation. For it is written: 'no one can

Lord!" who will enter the Kingdom of Heaven, but the one who does the will of my Father who is in heaven' (Mt. 7:21). And the Master specifies that it is not enough to invoke the Name of Jesus and, by its power, work wonders (prophesy, cast out demons), for he will say to them on the Day of Judgement: 'I never knew you.' Terrifying words!

The sanctifying invocation of the Name requires, primarily, the inner orientation of our will: to will what the Father wills – what he wills in heaven. What can he will if not to engender the Son, since he is nothing other than this engendering relationship? Such is the will of Mary: *fiat mihi secundum Verbum tuum*. 'According to thy Word': let what is effected in me be in conformity with the Form of forms, the Archetype of archetypes, with the Eternal Word which you engender in the unity of the Spirit. And also: 'may it be done unto me according to thy revelation, according to this Word of God which is Scripture.' Without this Marian *fiat mihi* there is no true comprehension of the Word, no exegesis or hermeneutic; only babbling, a prodigious babbling perhaps, a babbling provided with all of the scientific guarantees, but – and I mean this quite seriously – wind and chasing the wind. I fear that the Lord will declare to these babblers of exegesis – I too have occasionally been one – on the Day of Judgement: 'I never knew you.' For God can know and recognise only himself, that is to say those who bear his form, who have let themselves be informed according to his word, those who have been adorned with it, those who have not stifled it within themselves, but have delivered themselves up to its redemptive operation.

For this Word is operative, and is only one and the same operation – that of the unique Word and Redeemer: 'The unique Word formed of multiple sentences, each of which is a part of the same whole, of the same *Logos*.'[20] Only by this does the doctrine of the archetypal events assume its full significance, as

---

say "Jesus" but by the Spirit.' And seeing that the Name of Jesus is like the synthesis of the whole redemptive work (Jesus signifies 'God saves'), the hallowing of the Name is the model, the prototype of the whole work of grace, chiefly under its worship-related and scriptural form, as a sacralising 'informing' of the Christian soul.

[20] Origen, *Commentary on St John* 1:24.

will be shown presently. And, if Scripture is the Body of Christ, the Word 'made Book', the result is that it too participates in this Body's redemptive operation, just as the sacred events which it relates are, in the reality of the accomplished act, modes of participation in the work of salvation, modes according to which this work not only makes itself known, but also (by means of this very knowledge) is rendered efficacious and actualises, in a certain manner, what it signifies. For these events are events of grace, and this is what I would like to recall in concluding.

7. *On the metaphysical nature of human and divine-human acts*

I have spoken of archetypal events. But what is there of the archetypal in an event, that is, in the execution of an act or series of acts? Are these conditions external to its manifestation? As I have stated, these conditions, in what concerns the meta-historical phase of revelation, are, so to speak, inaccessible in themselves and can be known only by analogy. For the parahistorical phase, even though it takes place in a space–time setting, involves vanished modalities of earthly living conditions (a different geographic configuration and a slower passing of time). But the intrinsic reality of an act – unity of intention and execution – does not stem from its existential conditioning. It is of another order, that of *acting*, which is just as easily distinguished from the order of sensible things (a tree, a mountain, water, etc.) as from the order of intelligibles. What is then an act's mode of reality?

I say that it consists in the voluntary actualisation of a possibility; which is to say that it causes the intelligible to descend into existence (to whatever level on which this existence is situated) and renders it present there. Before the act has been accomplished, one cannot know if the possibility (in itself) is possible with respect to such and such an existential conditioning.[21] The act itself, ever risky, is the only proof of it. But, conversely, an accomplished act is never the definitive and total

---

[21] We need to distinguish the intrinsically possible (non-contradiction) from the extrinsically possible (the compatibility of such and such a possible with such and such conditions of realisation). For example, a straight line is intrinsically possible, but, in a curved universe, it is (extrinsically) impossible.

actualisation of the possible, and this is by virtue of the discontinuity between the principal order of the possibilities in itself – or the absolute possibilities – and the relative, changing order of their realisation. In itself a possibility is universal, an act is singular. There is, however, something of the definitive in the order of acting, and this is the first or inaugural act. It is this act which *opens* a way, which clears a passage for the descent of the possibility into the order of existence. Having opened this order to the realisation of the possibility, it modifies it, transforms it in such a way that the human milieu will 'call for', will 'require', if one may say so, the repetition of this realisation.[22] What has been done will be done. Each of our acts is thus responsible for a generating of analogous acts. This is why we should act according to the ways of Tradition, because they have been traced out following the will of God, and therefore following the order and the nature of things; whereas a completely new act, except in response to a divine initiative opening a new possibility in the tissue of reality, precipitates to some extent a whole series of other acts, risking an increase in the disorder of the world. Our acts are not innocent, nor without efficacy. They do not vanish with time like the wake of an ocean liner, but permanently and objectively modify the psychophysical continuum in which we live.[23]

It is in this sense that the events of Sacred History are archetypal events. They are all formed by inaugural acts which then open onto later possibilities for negative or positive realisation: possibilities of loss (original sin and all its consequences); possibilities of salvation (the redemptive work of Christ and the grace of the Sacraments, which are in themselves, in their principle, only archetypal acts of Christ, *ex opere operato* modes

---

[22] Our guide here is the model of the 'propagation of neural pathways' in the neo-cortex. We know that the interconnections of the cortical cells are only partially bestowed at birth. It is the experiences lived by the subject and the responses elaborated which contribute to the establishment and development of the neural network. Each primal experience and each primal act thus leaves an indelible trace, opening new pathways in the potential cerebral tissue. Moreover, the human world or cultural milieu is truly a social 'brain', from which the individual brain is obviously inseparable.

[23] These remarks are not unrelated to the law of increasing entropy; cf. my *La charité profanée*, pp. 55–63.

for the passage and the effusion of God's grace). We could for that matter distinguish different kinds of inaugurality in terms of the various phases of sacred history: an act can be inaugural for all of creation; or for human creation alone; or for a single people;[24] and within these phases we also need to consider relative degrees of primordiality, for history is not a quantitative accumulation of similar events, but a hierarchical series.

Conclusion: Christ the unity of the Alpha and the Omega

We see then that, in Christ, history itself, without ceasing to be history, is reunited with the metahistorical reality of the beginning. For these archetypal events of the Christ-epic have validity for a creation which groans as a whole in expectation of the Parousia, that is, the universal 'presence' of the Son of Man; and should not the Good News be preached to every creature? Here the world hesitates, here history turns in on itself, here time rolls itself up anew at the Tree of the Cross, the Tree of Life and the torch of light out of which the rays of vivifying glory blaze forth; here each letter of Holy Writ is ignited with the spark of the Holy Spirit and all of Scripture bursts into flame – that Burning Bush of revelation which burns without being consumed for ever and ever.[25]

---

[24] There is in fact something inaugural in every act: both because it shares in the primordiality of the act which it repeats (we have all sinned in Adam), and because it is never just a repetition, on account of the qualitative difference of every moment of time and history.

[25] Do I need to stress that this image specifically shows the relationship which unites Mary (identified with the Burning Bush in Patristic tradition) and Scripture? She gives to her Son his Body of flesh, just as Holy Writ gives him his scriptural Body. It is in fact in the Burning Bush that God reveals his Name, his Word. And just as Scripture is enkindled, inexhaustibly, by the Name of the Word, by that which is the synthesis of all revelation, so Mary bears the man Jesus, the perfection of all humanity, without harm to her inexhaustible virginity.

Part III

THE REDISCOVERED LIFE OF FAITH: THE DEIFYING GLORY

Chapter 11

The Scriptural and Theological Roots of Deification

The ultimate glory to which God destines every human creature is called 'deification'. Deification fulfils the promises inscribed in the sense of the supernatural; it actualises our integration with the risen Body of Christ. This notion, which plays such an important role in Eastern Christianity, is by no means absent in the Latin West. St Thomas treats of it in the light shed by Dionysius the Areopagite. Meister Eckhart confers on it its most forceful expression. However, to express its most orthodox foundations, I will turn to a masterpiece of French mysticism, Mgr Louis Laneau's treatise entitled *On the Deification of the Just*, convinced that the principles of our union with God should be expressed in a clearer and more orthodox way. Only material indispensable to my purpose will be quoted.[1]

1. Baptismal initiation and divine filiation

The Christian doctrine of deification is based on the ideas of filiation or sonship and adoption. These ideas are well known, but conceal an easily missed transcendent meaning, a meaning Mgr Laneau discovered one day in the course of what can only be called an illumination:

> In the course of prayer I happened upon these words of St John: *See what love the Father has given us, that we should be called*

[1] Laneau, a French missionary, wrote his treatise in Latin (*De deificatione justorum per Jesum Christum*) in Siam in 1693. A manuscript for many years, it was first published in 1887 (Hong Kong: Typis Societatis Missionum ad Exteros). In 1993, Jean-Claude Chenet published a very accurate translation of the first part of this text (*De la déification des justes*, Geneva: Ad Solem). With some slight changes, I have retained the version used for the first edition of *Le sens du surnaturel*, in 1986.

sons of God; and so we are! (I Jn. 3:1). Suddenly, either by chance or Providence, I communed with the sublime eloquence of the apostle's words. And my spirit, as if struck by an unexpected bolt of lightning, immediately began to have a presentiment and almost to divine that there was, in what the Evangelist was teaching, something far more lofty and far more divine than I had ever supposed. (p. 50)[2]

Laneau then decided to search both Scripture and the Greek and Latin Fathers. With his inspiration serving him as an Aladdin's lamp, he discovered scriptural and doctrinal treasures which he had previously overlooked. And so he came upon this statement of St Peter: 'He has granted us his precious and very great promises, that through these you may . . . become partakers of the divine nature [*divinæ naturæ consortes*]' (II Pet. 1:4):

> Is it possible to confer a more precious good on us than that of being rendered participants, not in power, not in knowledge, nor in any other perfection which may be found in God, but in *the divine nature itself*, above which there is nothing? By this we are in fact admitted into the community of God and, to use the customary language of the holy Fathers, we are transformed into God and conformed to him; we are deified. Now, since this clearly cannot occur according to nature, it is the effect of grace. But (and here we need to be most attentive) I am speaking of a grace which is a *quality*, that quality which, as St Cyril says, should be called *the quality* of God. And this is nothing other than participation in the divine nature, in other words, human deification. And most assuredly I am not uttering empty words, for all Catholics believe and teach that no one can be saved unless one has this quality. Thus St Dionysius clearly teaches (chapter eight of the *Ecclesiastical Hierarchy*) that no one can be saved if he does not obtain deification: 'There is no other salvation', he says, 'unless those who seek salvation become gods; now deification is the likeness of God, in as much as it is possible to resemble him; this is fusion with him, this is in a word the realisation of unity [*unitio*].' (pp. 83–4)[3]

---

[2] The bracketed numbers refer to the pages of Jean-Claude Chenet's French edition.

[3] The reference given by Laneau is inexact. The text is to be found in chap. 1 of *The Ecclesiastical Hierarchy* (PG 3, 373c). We can see here that Guénon's distinction between salvation and deliverance should not be used. All of these questions are treated in my book *Ésotérisme guénonien et mystère chrétien* (Lausanne: L'Age d'Homme, 1997).

Next Laneau proceeds to a study of the idea of adoption:

Everyone knows that, in ordinary language, adoption excludes generation, and conversely, generation excludes adoption. One can never say that a man has *adopted* his naturally engendered children. One speaks of adoption only where there has been no generation. And yet Scripture, contrary to our ordinary use of language, indiscriminately names as adoptive children those very ones it says are engendered and born of God ... For this to be the case, there has to be both true generation and true adoption at the same time.

First of all, I have already more than adequately shown that we are rendered sons of God by a true generation. However, should someone refuse to accept this, there is still a final and most persuasive argument to be found in the very definition of the nature of generation. By common consent generation is defined as *origination from a living being with likeness of nature*. Unquestionably, this definition also applies to regeneration. In fact, when we are reborn in baptism, we are born of a living being, born of God living and true: *they are born of God*. And on the other hand, we are also living beings by participation in his life since, as Scripture says, *And I live, yet not I, but Christ liveth in me* and *Our life is hid with Christ in God*.

We are, moreover, born in the likeness of the divine nature, because what is born of the Spirit is spirit, and because participation in the divine nature is bestowed on us (and this is that *new being* in which, according to St Thomas, we are formed); and we participate in accordance with a certain likeness to the divine nature, through the mode of generation or creation, as the same author teaches ...

Now it must be pointed out that nothing in this is opposed to what may be called adoptive sonship. In fact Scripture does not use this term to exclude notions of true filiation and true generation, but to distinguish it from the filiation of the divine Word. (p. 93)

For ourselves, it is uniquely by the will of the Father that we are called to things supernatural. It is different for the Son: the Son is God not just because the Father has willed it, but, having been engendered from the very substance of the Father, sonship is proper to him as his rightful estate and according to his very nature. As for ourselves, we are sons only by adoption, through likeness and in imitation of the Unique Son who is truly the Son. In essence our adoption consists in our receiving the power to become sons and to be born of God. And so the power we have received does not prevent our really being born of God, because the one precedes

The Sense of the Supernatural

and the other follows. Thus adoption, which is nothing other than this power, far from suppressing the notion of regeneration, precedes it as the cause it effects. It is impossible to be engendered and born of God if we have not first received adoption, that is to say the power to be born. (p. 94)

There is a great difference then between human and divine adoption; a difference defined by Laneau, still basing himself on St Thomas:

Human adoption is only an extrinsic benefit, thanks to which a family takes on the responsibility for a stranger by adopting him. He is said to be the son of such a family and is appointed as inheritor, without any physical generation and without anything intrinsic being involved, but purely by designation and in an extrinsic sense. This is why, between those adopting and the one adopted, no real relation can result, but only a relation of reason. With divine adoption, on the other hand, God does not take us to himself solely in an extrinsic way in order to confer glory on us, as the heretics think.[4] Rather, he does so in a real and intrinsic way, which is to say by the infusion of sanctifying grace which, as the Fathers say, establishes us in the divine nature, assimilates us to God as much as this is possible, and renders us sharers in the Holy Spirit. And since all this is accomplished through the mode of generation and birth, as I have abundantly demonstrated, it follows that between ourselves and the God who adopts us there is a true and real relationship which, as is said in philosophical language, has its own basis in a true and real regeneration or 'justification'. This is why we are not only called sons, but are said to be *born* of God. This could never be said of an adopted child.

Finally, let us not forget the teaching of St Thomas: in so far as all that is accomplished in time is an image of what has been for all eternity, filiation by adoption is evidently like an image of natural and eternal filiation. In conclusion, let us state with the holy Doctor that, although divine adoption is common to the entire Trinity, it can be appropriated to the Father as to its author, to the Son as to its exemplar, and to the Holy Spirit as to the one who imprints within us the likeness of this exemplar. (pp. 95–7)

---

[4] This is a reference to the Lutheran doctrine of extrinsic or 'forensic' justification; cf. Chapter 5 above.

Scriptural and Theological Roots of Deification

2. *Eucharistic initiation and Christification*

The primary basis for deification is that we become, through baptism, children of God, and hence born of the Father. Scripture reveals the second basis, which is that we are *members of the Body of Christ* and by this means united to Christ. Now, if the sacramental act which confers on us the dignity of being children of God is baptism, the sacramental act which incorporates us into Christ is Eucharistic communion. This is what nourishes and develops the grace of adoption and, in man, actualises an image of the hypostatic union, the union of the divine and human in the unique hypostasis (= person) of the Word:

> Just as Christ by the hypostatic union possesses the divine life which is proper to God, for all that is with God is communicated to Christ's human nature; so also we ourselves, when restored by Christ's Body and Blood, are rendered one with him, sharers in the divine nature which is in him. This is why our life becomes the divine life of Christ, just as – but keeping everything in proportion – through the hypostatic union the life of human nature becomes the divine life. For this reason Jesus Christ himself has said: 'As the living Father sent me, and I live because of the Father, so he who eats me will live because of me' [Jn. 6:57]. It is all one and the same thing to say, on the one hand: I who am sent by the living Father live and bestow life on my humanity by virtue of this union; and on the other: to those who eat of me, because they are united and conjoined to me by my flesh, I will give them life. (pp. 119–20)

Next Laneau examines scriptural texts which speak of this unitive incorporation in Christ in a much more realistic way than he had previously imagined. In particular, he examines this saying of Christ reported by St John (17:21): 'That they may all be one; even as thou, Father, art in me, and I in thee, that they also may be in us.' He bases his commentary on St Hilary who, in his treatise *On the Trinity*,[5] provides an astonishing argument against those heretics who deny the divinity of Christ:

> When the heretics declare that the Son is not in the Father, unless by assent of his will, just as we are not one with and in Christ unless by agreement and the union of the heart, he [St Hilary] turns

[5] Bk. 8, chap. 2.

this argument against them and teaches that we are not only united with Christ by virtue of a consent of the will, but that this union is true and *natural*, as is proved by the Eucharist. By this it must be inferred that the union of the Son with the Father is equally *natural*. (p. 133)

Evidently we should not understand that, by this natural unity, we ourselves and Christ form a single natural being; such a doctrine would be unworthy of so great a doctor. But he only means that, in addition to the union that is realised within us by reason of charity, faith and the agreement of souls with Christ, Christ himself is present within us as a true and real presence. He is so because it is he who is the cause of charity, faith and grace. Besides, the holy Fathers quite often employ the words *natural* or *naturally* to designate, not what is symbolic or moral, or, as I have shown, what is dependent upon the mind and will, but with regard to what is real, true and founded in things themselves, and in no way dependent upon the mind and will of men. (p. 134)

Look then and see just where St Hilary's argument leads us, he who has not hesitated to prove a most sublime thing, namely Christ's divinity, with the help of another and no less obscure and difficult thing, namely our union with Christ in the Eucharist. But this is not surprising because, in those times, faith in the Eucharist and the virtues was firm and not an object of controversy among the faithful. (p. 136)

3. *Paracletic initiation and spiritual perfection*

Laneau turns next to this same doctrine of unity in Christ as it is found in the works of St Cyril of Alexandria. This saint distinguishes three kinds of union with Christ: a union of love; a union by the Eucharist (which he calls *corporeal* or *natural* union), and a union by the Holy Spirit (which he calls spiritual). These three kinds of union actualise not only the real unity of man and Christ, but also the real unity of the just among themselves, who thus become members of each other. This work of unification is accomplished not only by the communion of Christians in the same Eucharistic body – according to the words of St Paul, *one bread, one body* – but also and especially by the Holy Spirit. And so we are led directly to an examination of the third basis for deification revealed by Scripture: not only are we *members of the Mystical Body*, but we are even *temples of the Holy Spirit*. Here we have one of the major themes of

Scriptural and Theological Roots of Deification

Laneau's treatise.[6] Someone once asked St Seraphim of Sarov what the goal of the Christian life was. He replied: the acquisition of the Holy Spirit. This is because the presence of the Holy Spirit in the being of the just is unique, even when compared to the presence of the other two Persons of the Trinity. Let us recall that theology distinguishes between a natural presence of God (according to three modes: by his Essence, by his Power and by his Infinity) and a supernatural presence according to the gifts of grace. But the presence of the Holy Spirit is even more profound:

> By the term *indwelling* [of the Holy Spirit] we must not understand that assistance of the Holy Spirit through which, by virtue of the divine immensity, he is present to all things, nor even the presence which implies his operation, the infusion of grace or supernatural gifts; but rather that union, both internal and real, that coming of the Holy Spirit into the soul by which the just, apart from the graces and gifts with which the Holy Spirit adorns them, possess *the very Person of the Holy Spirit*, living and dwelling in each of them. This is a truth so firm and so assured that if, against all probability (as the theologians say), the Holy Spirit were not everywhere through his immensity, he would nevertheless be in the just soul informed by his grace. By grace he in fact is inclined to manifest his most perfect presence in such a soul, thus uniting himself to this soul in the most perfect manner possible. What is involved here is not just a union of the affective order, or one uniting us to a known and loved object, for both of these may be encountered even between persons separated from each other. Nor is this a natural union like the one existing between body and soul; still less is it a metaphorical union, for this would be nominal or merely analogical. How then can we describe this union? Surely as ineffable, far exceeding our grasp, yet most real and most true. By it the Person of the Holy Spirit, communicating himself as such to the just person, deifies and informs him with supernatural life much like the soul informs the body. Theologians do not hesitate to say that this union is roughly analogous to the hypostatic union. (pp. 147–8)

---

[6] Evidently this indwelling of the Holy Spirit can be seen as corresponding to the sacrament of confirmation. One can speak then of a triple deification: relative to the Father (baptism), to the Son (the Eucharist) and to the Holy Spirit (confirmation).

With respect to the human person, we see then that the Holy Spirit plays the same role that the soul plays, on a natural plane, with respect to the body – but in a supernatural mode. Just as the soul informs the body, communicating natural life to it, so also the Holy Spirit informs the deified person, communicating divine life. In some way he becomes the soul of the soul. Laneau enumerates many passages where Scripture speaks of the indwelling of the Holy Spirit, and then concludes:

> From these testimonies, and others like them, theologians have drawn the following conclusion (St Thomas Aquinas, *Summa Theologiae* Ia, 43): even though the Holy Spirit may be said to be 'sent' in relation to the gift of grace, yet it must be so understood that, by grace, the soul is disposed to enter into possession of the divine Person, the Holy Spirit. As a result, if the Holy Spirit is sent, this is so that he may be given to us and that we should possess him, that his divine Person may be ours, that it might belong to us, that we should freely enjoy this same Person as a rightful good, and that it might dwell within us. Therein lies the significance of the words *that the Holy Spirit be given* and *to possess the Holy Spirit*. And indeed this same Angelic Doctor has no difficulty in admitting that it would be false to say that the Person of the Holy Spirit is not given to us, but that we only receive his gifts.
>
> Besides, Sacred Scripture itself teaches that the Holy Spirit should be in us as in a temple. First of all, Christ the Lord himself, in whom *dwelleth all the fulness of the Godhead corporeally*, calls his body a temple: *Destroy (solvite) this temple ... he was speaking of the temple of his body*. As for ourselves, we are called temples of God by virtue of the indwelling of the Holy Spirit within us, and so we are. Quite often the Apostle speaks in this way: *Know ye not, that your members are the temple of the Holy Spirit, who is in you, whom you have from God?* Let us note in passing that St Paul almost never makes use of the expression *know ye not* (which is as much a warning and a reprimand as a reference to doctrine), except when he clearly feels that the human spirit, which is minimally inclined to think of anything beyond sense experience, requires harsh words to rouse it from its ancient slumber. He does this, however, when he teaches that we are temples of the Holy Spirit, that we are members of Jesus Christ, etc....
>
> And we should not pass over this in silence: even though the Most Holy Trinity dwells within us as well as the Holy Spirit, according to this word of the Lord: *We shall come to him and make our abode with him*, it remains, however, a prevailing custom

among holy authors to call us temples of the Holy Spirit rather than of the Most Holy Trinity. Without doubt this is because the work of our sanctification is commonly attributed to him, but also and above all because, as is clearly seen in the scriptural texts quoted above, the Person of the Holy Spirit is so completely given to us that if – which is impossible – he could be separated from the Father and the Son, these two Persons not coming to us, the Holy Spirit would still come and dwell in us.

Yes, he comes, not in the manner of a traveller or a runner from the highways, but as master of the house and as one who intends to stay and abide. He comes to his own, in his own house. (pp. 150–2)

4. *The deifying operations*

Now we come to the second part of Laneau's work, dedicated to spiritual methodology. The practices and exercises imposed on those wishing to embark on the way of deification are envisaged from a triple point of view: from the point of view of filiation, from the point of view of incorporation and from the point of view of paracletic indwelling. It is possible moreover – Laneau himself speaks of it to some degree – to relate this triple distinction to the three stages of the spiritual way, the stages of the beginner, the proficient and the perfect. In the first we are *born* to deification; in the second we *grow*; and in the third we are *completed* in Christ. This way is quite different to the idea which some have formed of Christian mysticism.[7] It involves no phenomena, no visions, no ecstasies, no special revelations. Essentially it amounts to a continual exercise of concentration on Christ: to act, love, think and be 'in Christ'. This long and habitual concentration produces 'the influx of the spirit of Christ in a normal way'. And a sure sign of this influx is that 'during prayer' the Spirit comes to pray within us 'in a way impossible to describe'.

Commenting on St Paul's various formulas for life 'in Christ', Laneau comes upon the injunction for us to 'walk with him' (Col. 2:6), an injunction which he had already encountered in the first part and which he explains in this way:

---

[7] René Guénon in particular.

We walk with Christ when, advancing from virtue to virtue, we labour to define and form Christ himself within us in the most perfect manner (but, because we always have the tendency to fall, the Apostle enjoins us not to be discouraged); so that we should remain always in Christ, like strollers in a garden who never pause to do anything, but advance from place to place, without for all that going outside the enclosure.... And in fact, if someone walks in the garden, he is never idle, but goes by various paths wherever his soul leads him; sometimes the beauty of the flowers ravishes him, sometimes the sweetness of the fruits nourishes him, and yet he never leaves. In just this way we too are always walking in Christ. (p. 166)[8]

Without Christ we can do nothing. The extraordinary nobility of our spiritual destiny, called as we are to share in the divine nature, goes hand in hand with the certitude of our own nothingness. Laneau describes this nothingness, this nihility (*nihilitas*) in a manner reminiscent of Meister Eckhart:

Numerous are they who do not immediately perceive the reason why we cannot, by ourselves, have access to God; this is why I will briefly mention that our alienation [*alienatio*] from God, for all that we can judge of it, comes not only from the demerits of our sins, but stems above all from our nihility [*nihilitas*] and the infinity of the divine. And in fact, since God is infinite by nature, whereas creatures are finite, it follows that God himself is both All and all things, while compared to him creatures are nothing, or almost nothing. Thus, in going from the creature to God, there can be neither proportion nor access. For, if creatures were something, if they possessed some reality which was not from God or in God, then God would be limited by such a separate reality ...; if such were the case God would no longer be either infinite according to all manner of being and perfection, or absolutely infinite. (p. 173)

What then is the reality of creatures? What is their nature? If we regard creatures as being outside of God, they will appear to have some substance; but, if we consider them as being in God, then this entire reality is nothing but sheer dependency with respect to him, a relationship no different from that which unites the ray to the sun. Considered in itself, the ray is something; but, compared to the sun, it is hardly anything, if indeed it can be distinguished

---

[8] Henceforth the bracketed numbers refer to the second part (pp. 165–430) of the Latin edition of *De deificatione* (Hong Kong: Typis Societatis Missionum ad Exteros, 1887).

from the sun at all, for it cannot be conceived of except as an effusion streaming from it. (pp. 173–5)

Laneau also asks himself what reading – apart from the Holy Gospels – is appropriate for those engaged in the way of deification. In his opinion, far too many authors confidently offer to teach us about Christ, but only do so with the help of long and subtle reasonings. What is more, their pages ignore the Name of Jesus, which they seem to mention only under duress, whereas St Bernard teaches that no book has any savour for him if it lacks the Name of Jesus: 'Jesus, honey in the mouth, music in the ear, jubilation in the heart':

> So much for St Bernard. The same goes for that small book, *The Imitation of Christ*, which is universally recommended. It speaks of nothing save Jesus; it resounds with nothing but the Name of Jesus.... But let us see how St Paul expresses himself in his epistles. Everywhere we find Jesus, everywhere Christ. There is scarcely a short verse or even a single line in which he has not placed the Name of Jesus, often more than once. When he develops a certain argument, if perchance the Name of Jesus occurs beneath his pen, he immediately abandons its development and, in the ecstasy of his soul, is borne to Jesus. For a spirit inebriated with God and Christ no longer knows any measure, no longer exhales any other breath than that of Jesus Christ, no longer utters any other cry than Jesus. (p. 236)

To conclude, I offer a text in which it is perhaps possible to recognise, if not the actual secret of what the author himself has experienced, at least an echo of that experience, taken from a section in which Laneau examines the kinds of prayer and meditation proper for each of the stages of the spiritual way:

> Concerning the prayer of the perfect, it does not behove us to say anything; they are heavenly eagles who fly so high that they escape our gaze. *Their life is hid with Christ* (Col. 3:3). This is why the *psychic man* (I Cor. 2:14) has no right to say what he would consider suitable about it.... The former live with God, in God, and, *with face unveiled, contemplating the glory of the Lord*, they are transformed *into this same image* (II Cor. 3:18). And Christ the Lord, who is the *image of the Father* (Col. 1:15) and the *figure of his substance* (Heb. 1:3), by multiple and successive irruptions into their spirit, glorifies them with a light always new, and by

marvellous and unheard-of fulgurations, leads them ceaselessly towards ever more glory. And this is why they go bounding among the *mountains* and leaping over the *hills* of our concepts (Song of Songs 2:17). The Holy Spirit quickens and inflames and consumes them with his fire. (pp. 421–2)

Chapter 12

From Deification to Creation

1. *Theology or mysticism?*

The mystery of deification completes what is only remotely and obscurely anticipated by the sense of the supernatural, a foreknowledge of which is inscribed in the very substance of our being but only consummated by grace. In this mystery resides the essence of the Christian revelation: 'God has been made man so that man might become God', as St Augustine so admirably declares in an oft-repeated formula.[1] This doctrine, kept alive in the Christian East to this day, expounded in the West by the greatest of the theologians and mystics, has almost completely vanished from modern Catholicism. Present-day bishops seem much more haunted by cares about unemployment, racism and war than by a concern for deifying glory. But it is often the same for a neo-Thomism which is suspicious of pantheism and is above all concerned with preserving God from any 'entitative contact'. Not only do these two attitudes coincide, but the latter attitude bears some responsibility for the former.

At best, both camps allow the mystics the right to hyperbole. But they keep careful watch lest their statements be given any 'ontological' interpretation, dismissing them as excesses of language lacking any metaphysical import. In connection with St John of the Cross and his doctrine of the soul's participation in the life of the Trinity, Maritain explains: 'Clearly, once again, the saint is not using the language of the speculative theologian; there is absolutely no question here, from any point of view, of an *entitative* participation of the creature in the uncreated act of love by reason of which the Holy Spirit proceeds from the

---

[1] 'Factus est Deus homo ut homo firet Deus', Sermon 128, *PL* 39, 1997; a Christmas sermon.

Father and the Son.'² And later, in the same text, he specifies that the soul, 'crowned with the seven gifts, penetrates to the bosom of the Trinitarian life without the essence of the Three undergoing, or ever being able to undergo, the slightest *entitative* contact.'³ But the saint says exactly the opposite:

> The soul ... is no longer satisfied with the knowledge and communication of the 'back' of God – which was his communication to Moses [Exod. 33:23] – and which is knowledge of him in his effects and works; she can only be satisfied with God's face, which is an essential communication of the divinity to the soul. This communication is not brought about through any means, but through a certain contact of the soul with the divinity. This contact is something foreign to everything sensory and accidental, since it is a touch of naked substances – of the soul and the divinity.⁴

If such phraseology seems incompatible with the language of theology, it is by no means certain that it is the mystic who should give way; perhaps it is theological language which should lend an ear to a better-informed authority. Not that procedures suitable for the understanding should be denied, or that they be seen only as initial steps toward a provisional apprehension. But we cannot identify the whole of the intellect with such a philosophical practice. It is always the understanding itself which knows, but this understanding necessarily restricts the horizon of the possible to objects within its experience. Now the mystic has encountered realities which, by their very presence, specifically teach him that there are possibilities of being other than those customarily imagined by a conventional philosopher. When the intellect has such an experience, it endures no violation of its own needs. On the contrary, each illumination, by enlarging it, fulfils it and reveals unsuspected or as yet 'unrecognised' perfections within it. If the intellect could perceive its own luminous essence, nothing would prove astonishing or surprising to it. But it does not possess such a knowledge naturally. Its cognitive capacity has to be actualised

---

² *The Degrees of Knowledge* trans. (under the supervision of G. B. Phelan) (New York: Scribners, 1959), p. 376; Maritain's emphasis.
³ Ibid., p. 377; author's emphasis.
⁴ *The Spiritual Canticle*, stanza 19, 4; *The Collected Works of St John of the Cross* (Washington, DC: ICS Publications, 1973), p. 486.

From Deification to Creation

by the object received within itself, and only in this way does it become aware of its own truth and capacity, which is in a certain manner infinite, because united to the divine Light. As St John of the Cross says,

> The soul upon which the divine light of God's being is ever shining, or better, in which it is always dwelling by nature, is like [a] window ... A man makes room for God by wiping away all the smudges and smears of creatures, by uniting his will perfectly to God's; for to love is to labour to divest and deprive oneself for God of all that is not God. When this is done the soul will be illumined by and transformed into God. And God will so communicate his supernatural being to it that it will appear to be God himself and will possess all that God himself has.[5]

Scripture too seems to ignore certain precautions of language. Christ's response to the Jews who accused him of claiming to be God was a quotation from Psalm 82:6: 'I say, You are gods.' And the echo of this is found in St Peter's statement – the most explicit in all of Scripture – at the beginning of his second epistle: 'Christ hath called us to his own proper glory and virtue', that is, to become 'partakers of the divine nature'. Certainly, very few theologians are inclined to express themselves spontaneously in such terms. And likewise St John the Apostle underscores, as we have seen, the truth and reality of our divine filiation: 'that we should be called children of God; and so we are' (I Jn. 3:1).[6] St Irenaeus recapitulates all this in stating: 'The Word of God, Jesus Christ Our Lord, ... because of his superabundant love, has been made exactly like us so that we may be made exactly like him.'[7]

We should not be surprised then to rediscover among Western mystics such images as the immersion of the soul in the divine Ocean, a symbolism which seems typically Oriental. Thus, St Alphonsus de Liguori writes: 'In spiritual marriage, the soul is transformed in God and becomes simply *one* with him, as a vessel

---

[5] *The Ascent of Mount Carmel*, bk. 2, chap. 5, 6–7; *Collected Works*, p. 117.

[6] *Translator's Note:* The French is much more emphatic: 'Nous sommes appelés: fils de Dieu. Et nous le sommes!' – We are called: sons of God. And such we are!

[7] *Against the Heresies*, prologue to bk. 5.

of water, when emptied into the sea, becomes simply one with it' (*Homo apostolicus*, app. 1, no. 18). St Teresa of Avila, speaking of the highest state of union (in this life), declares that it happens like 'rain falling from the heavens into a river or a spring; there is nothing but water there and it is impossible to divide or separate the water belonging to the river from that which fell from the heavens.' And again, 'it is as if a tiny streamlet enters the sea, from which it will find no way of separating itself, or as if in a room there were two large windows through which the light streamed in: it enters in through different places but it all becomes one' (*Interior Castle*, Seventh Mansion, chap. 2).

Should these analogies, which under an Eastern pen would readily pass for unqualified pantheism, be regarded as the overflowings of a soul more attentive to the fervour of its spiritual state than cautious about speculative exactness? Not at all, for if they sin, it is by deficiency and not by excess. In the prologue to *The Living Flame of Love*, St John of the Cross tells us: 'Everything that I will say is infinitely below what in reality occurs in this intimate union of the soul with God.'

2. 'As I will be known, I will know'

How then to express this paradox of a 'fusion without confusion' of the soul with God? How can a given reality be totally transformed into another without for all that ceasing to be itself?

The first response to such a question is provided by intellectual activity. The intellect in fact unites with what is not itself, receives its object into itself and, in this openness to what is other, realises its own nature. This is why the fine point of the intellect, which is also the heart and centre of the being, called 'the spirit of the soul' by St Teresa of Avila, is considered by theology to be the 'place' of deification, that place where the divine Essence unites with created being and becomes the very act of its intellect, just as the luminosity of a crystal is solely the activity of sunlight. The divine Being actualises the heart-intellect which is resplendent with an uncreated Light.

> The soul will be illumined by and transformed in God. And God will so communicate his supernatural being to it that it will appear to be God himself . . . so great a union is caused that all the things of both God and the soul become one in participant transformation,

and the soul appears to be more God than a soul. Indeed, it is God by participation. Yet truly, its being (even though transformed) is naturally as distinct from God's as it was before, just as the window, although illumined by the ray, has an existence distinct from the ray.[8]

Indeed, there is here an identity of intellection (of the divine Essence) with its object (the divine Essence). But, for this Essence to become the cognitive act of the human intellect, it is clearly necessary that, in its pure luminous essence, this intellect be basically identical with the light of the divine Intellect: the luminosity of the crystal is indistinguishable from the light which actuates it, and the light is identical within itself and in the crystal which it renders luminous. But within itself the crystal obviously remains distinct from the light passing through it. Knowledge of the divine Essence basically consists in this: that God is the knowledge in the very act of our intellection, which refers to the divine Word according to the statement in St Luke: 'No one knoweth ... who the Father is, but the Son, and to whom the Son will reveal him' (10:22); and also Psalm 35:10: 'In thy light we shall see light.' In this cognitive act, then, the intellect realises its identity with its prototype *in divinis*, its identity with the Idea which God, from all eternity, has formed of this intellect. The beatific vision which the 'deified' intellect has of the divine Essence cannot, in the last analysis, be anything but that vision which the divine Essence itself has of this intellect. According to St Thomas, do not creatures have in God an 'uncreated being', as I have elsewhere noted?[9] Now, is not this uncreated being, which is the Idea or archetype which God forms of the creature in his Word or Knowledge of himself, equally and necessarily the mode according to which God allows himself to be partaken of by creatures? Is not the 'form' in which or according to which God sees the creature also the 'form' according to which the glorified creature sees God? Is there any other way to understand this text from St Paul: 'For those whom he foreknew, he also predestined to be made conformable to the image of his Son;

---

[8] *The Ascent of Mount Carmel*, bk. 2, chap. 5, 6–7; *Collected Works*, p. 117.

[9] *La charité profanée* (Bouère: Editions Dominique Martin Morin, 1979), p. 342.

that he might be the first-born among many brothers. And those whom he predestined, he also called. And those whom he called, he also glorified' (Rom. 8:29–30)? Confronted with this text, how can anyone deny that the foreknowledge which God has of the creature in his Word who is the Form of forms, a foreknowledge which is thus identical with the archetype of the creature, also governs the final glorification of this same creature? This is summarised elsewhere in St Paul: 'As I will be known, I will know' (I Cor. 13:12).

3. The uncreated Mystery within us

Does all this involve the literal identification of the creature's substantial being with God? Certainly not. The created being as such remains a created being, and never 'becomes' the Creator. If we express ourselves in this way, it is not only to 'safeguard' divine transcendence – 'precautionary' thinking makes for poor metaphysics – but rather because it is philosophically absurd to suppose that what truly existed once might no longer exist some day. Deification is not an eraser to bring about the creature's obliteration. The highest identification, sometimes called the 'supreme identity', should not exclude supreme distinctiveness, it should not be tantamount to a vanishing of the immortal person into a broadly homogeneous Absolute – a kind of ontological 'black hole' – with which it is all too often confused. And this, once again, is not the result of the well-known and obstinate Western desire to preserve one's being, but because, whenever this involves a true being, every complete annihilation of being is purely and simply inconceivable. Now, however far we may go in declaring the nothingness of the creature – and I will certainly go as far as anyone in this direction – we should not end up with the creature's total non-existence, since, if the creature's non-existence were absolute, we would hardly need to go so far as to declare its non-existence. Only what is nothing is annihilated, so that this annihilation is truly a realisation that only effaces an illusory appearance of being. But not everything in this appearance can be illusory. And illusion itself is not purely illusory, a mere nothing, otherwise it would not even exist as an illusion. The only way to make sense of all this is the concept of *relative reality*. Illusion does not lie in believing that the created world is real, but in believing it to be absolute Reality. And yet this is what every creature seems to proclaim.

A relative reality is a connected reality, or even a reality of 'relatedness'. The relation uniting the creature to God is real precisely because the reality of the creature is dependent upon this relation. Creation, says St Thomas, is a relation *in* the creature, which means that the creature's being is God-given.[10] But who receives this being? Or again: what is the creature independent of the gift of being? Theology answers: a possibility of creation, an essence in God. It is this essence which receives the gift of existence and which, in this very way, becomes a creature. And, in the case of man, this essence is 'in the image' of God, which is to say 'according to the Word' (or Son), the unique Image of the Father. This is why St Paul affirms that God 'is not far from each one of us, for in him we live and move and have our being . . . For we are indeed *his offspring*' (Acts 17:27–8). And yet we have to conform ourselves to this 'image' which is the mystery of the Uncreated in the created; we have to 'realise' it by becoming children of God in Christ in such a way that eternal Wisdom can cry out with Jesus: 'I said, you are gods' (Jn. 10:34). Therefore we believe that the partaking of the divine nature, spoken of in II Peter, which is realised by the grace of filial adoption in Jesus Christ, accomplishes the perfection already inscribed in original human nature. In other words and to speak more clearly, there is in the depths of created being, at its very core, in its most intimate heart, something uncreated and divine, 'for in order for something to partake of God', says St Gregory of Nyssa, 'it is indispensable to possess in its being something corresponding to the partaken'.[11]

But this immanence of the Uncreated in the created constitutes the very limit of the created; it is within it like something not itself, an opening, an interruption of finiteness itself, an ontological fissure of which man must indeed have a certain awareness. Unquestionably, we are far from the Aristotelian ontology in which scholastic philosophy found the wherewithal to establish the perfect consistency of the individual being. But

---

[10] *Summa Theologiae* Ia, 45, 3.
[11] *Oratio catechetica magna*, V; PG 45, 21c.

this ontology cannot as such account for the *created* nature of this being, still less for its ordination to the grace of divine filiation. It is quite necessary that this ordination to deification possess an ontological root in created being if we are not to lapse into unintelligible supernaturalism.

'Man', says St Basil, 'is a creature who has received the order to become God.' This saying, quoted by St Gregory Nazianzus,[12] is decisive for the destiny of human nature. But the realisation of this order, far from claiming to make the created equal to the Uncreated, on the contrary requires its effacement and an effective awareness of its complete dependence. And here I would like to interject the notion of obediential potency. If it is true that man is a creature who has received the order to become God, he must actually possess the power to obey this order. Obediential potency,[13] which renders nature capable of supernature and of even a purely divine existence (this is so for the human nature assumed by the eternal Word), is the infinite power of infinite obedience. And this is why it is prototypically realised as such in the Virgin Mary, who is *obedience made creature*, a truly ontological obedience, which realises the truth of created being. The Virgin is the purest creature because she is most purely a creature, which is defined as having a given being and therefore a received being: by itself a mere nothing with respect to the All. And her ontological annihilation, her virginal and immaculate *esse*, has merited for her the begetting of the Creator of the worlds and the very source of Being.

Likewise, that which is more than human in a human being is truly actualised only in proportion to its own effacement: 'He must increase and I must decrease,' as John the Baptist declares. Now, in the natural order, the intellective power is already a trace of the more than human, since, through the activity of the intellect (that is to say, through knowledge), a human being is open to all other beings which are thus able to

[12] *In laudem Basilii Magni*, Oratio xliii, §48, *PG* 36, 560a.
[13] This notion, classical in theology, designates the capacity which created nature must possess so as to *be able to obey* the supernatural orders given it by God, so as to accomplish operations beyond the strength of its nature. The Thomists see it as a passive power. Other theologians see it as a power that is both active and passive (Suarez). I am making use of it in an analogical and mystical sense.

From Deification to Creation

'exist' within him. By extending this natural datum, we can admit then that it is within man's intellective power, supernaturalised by the light of glory, to commune with the uncreated Light of divine Reality, for 'God is light'. And, with regard to this communion with light, St Teresa tells us: 'as far as one can understand, it is impossible to say more than that the soul, or rather the spirit of the soul, is made one with God.'[14] And St John of the Cross goes so far as to speak of a transformation into God:

> He [the Spouse] is the virtue of supreme humility, he loves you with supreme humility and esteem and makes you his equal, gladly revealing himself to you in these ways of knowledge, in his countenance filled with graces, and telling you in this his union, not without great rejoicing: 'I am yours and for you and delighted to be what I am so as to be yours and give myself to you' ... All that can be said of this stanza is less than the reality, for the transformation of the soul in God is indescribable. Everything can be expressed in this statement: the soul becomes God from God through participation in him and in his attributes.[15]

So also for St Thomas: 'We are gods by participation under the effect of grace.'[16] And St Maximus the Confessor affirms that human persons are called upon to reunite within themselves, 'through love, uncreated nature with created nature by causing them to appear in unity and identity in the acquisition of grace'.[17] But thus glorified, the intellect (the *spirit of the soul*, to use the phrase of St Teresa), is also and necessarily the heart of our being, the innermost of our interiority, that secret opening at the centre of our finiteness known only to God; which means that this supreme and deifying knowledge is only obtained by the renunciation of all knowledge, the renunciation of all activity proper to the intellect, so that God alone may be able to work within it. In such a perfectly despoiled intellect, the irruption of uncreated Light inundates and transfigures the entire being, envelops it with an aureole of glory. And this is what I think the last mystery of the Rosary, the Coronation of Mary, signifies.

---

[14] *Interior Castle*, Seventh Mansion, chap. 2.
[15] *The Living Flame of Love*, stanza 3, 5–8; *Collected Works*, pp. 612–14.
[16] *In Joannem*, 15, 2, 1.
[17] *Ambiguorum liber*, 41; PG 91, 1308b.

Does this then involve that 'entitative contact' between God and creature so strongly condemned by Maritain? Surely not, for properly speaking such a 'contact' is quite simply impossible. Every contact presupposes limits across which different realities can touch one another, while the divine Substance is limitless.[18] But, on the other hand, to imagine that the creature remains irremediably enclosed in its own finiteness is, in a certain manner, to consign it to hell. But is not this just what we are exposed to if we are allowed to think that the creature should in some way 'keep its distance' vis-à-vis God, as if this entitative contact were somehow possible after all, but something to which we had no right? In truth, to deny any entitative contact, while asserting that uncreated substance remains infinitely distant from created substances, is without doubt to express oneself in an acceptable way, a way which safeguards transcendence. But, in so doing, by establishing a relation of distance between God and man, we risk – as a seemingly paradoxical consequence – the ruination of transcendence. In reality, if I may say so, divine transcendence risks nothing. Adequately understood, divine Infinity does not exclude anything finite, for to do so would both leave the finite outside of itself and limit itself. By virtue of its limitlessness, divine Infinity includes all of the finite within itself. Only from the point of view of finite being is the Infinite outside. This is what, according to Father Sertillanges, St Thomas expresses 'in a surprising way', by declaring that God knows creatures in himself and not in themselves (*Summa Theologiae* Ia, 14, 5). Should we not conclude then that, as long as the creature is 'in itself', it will not be able to know God *as* it is known?

'In the Holy Spirit', writes the great St Athanasius, 'the Word glorifies the creature, and, by conferring deification and adoptive filiation upon it, leads it to the Father.'[19] For the creature to enter into the Spirit, it must let the Spirit enter through that ontological fissure, that open door at the heart of our created being through which God beholds us and beckons, and through

---

[18] When St John of the Cross speaks of 'a touch of naked substances', it is, then, a 'unilateral' contact from the side of human substance, but not from the side of divine substance – which is not unrelated to the 'sound of one hand clapping' spoken about in Zen Buddhism.

[19] *Epistula I ad Serapionem*, 25; PG 26, 589B.

From Deification to Creation

which is accomplished the mystery of our true identity; for, how can we be 'ourselves' other than by partaking of the only one who is truly himself? Meister Eckhart teaches that

> in created things there is no truth. There is something which transcends the created being of the soul, not in contact with created things, which are nothing; not even an angel has it, though he has a clear being that is pure and extensive: even that does not touch it. It is akin to the nature of deity, it is one in itself, and has nothing in common with anything. It is a stumbling-block to many a learned cleric. It is a strange and desert place, too unnameable to name, too unknown to know. If you could annihilate yourself for an instant, indeed I say less than an instant, you would possess all that this is in itself.... The Latin word *ego*, which means 'I', is proper to none but God in his oneness. The Latin word *vos* means 'you', you who are called to be one in unity. These two terms, *ego* and *vos*, I and you, thus both stand for unity.[20]

4. '*Fiat voluntas tua*'

For a certain kind of theology, however, such an annihilation is something impossible and contrary to the ontological fulness of the created. Either these formulations are excesses of language, manners of speaking, or mystics of the essence, of whom Meister Eckhart is the apex, sin by an unspeakable forgetfulness of the human being's irremediably created nature. We are cautioned to remember this and accept ourselves as such. Wise counsel, but infinitely more difficult to put into practice than surmised, and I think that only a mystic of the essence rightly lets us follow it through to its ultimate consequences.

Here we find a second 'locus' of deification complementary to the first, the 'locus' of the will. The crystalline point of the intellect lets us understand how the light can be infused within it and penetrate it totally. Created being as such remains, however, a kind of foreign body within this transforming immersion. Now deification cannot be restricted only to the powers of the soul; it is the king who is crowned and not his servants; it should speak to our very being. Our being must find that, in reality and to the very extent that it is a creature, it

---

[20] Sermon 17: 'Ego elegi vos de mundo'; *Traités et Sermons*, trans. Alain de Libera (Paris: Garnier/Flammarion, 1993), pp. 325–6.

is 'at home' here in its rightful kingdom. For this there is no alternative but to go all the way to the end of created nature, which can only be accomplished in the mystery of the will. The reason for this is that, while the intellect is the recipient within us of what we are not, the will is involved with the most personal aspect of our being and is its direct expression.

The fundamental law of the human being, as we have frequently noted, is that it should become what it is, that it should realise its essence. But, in accordance with its nature, this is a double realisation. It is not enough – dare I say it – to realise our deiformity; we also need to realise our status as creature, which is in a certain manner identified with our will. And all I want to emphasise here is that, contrary to what is ordinarily thought, the actual realisation of our status as creatures, far from being a natural datum, is conditioned by the realisation of our deiformity according to this saying of Christ: 'Seek ye therefore first the kingdom of God and his justice, and all these things shall be added unto you.' But to go from a passively endured to an actively assumed state of creaturehood demands a complete conversion of the will.

Through the intellect we grasp the uncreated Light and identify ourselves with it. But the intellective mirror possesses an obscure face, a 'tenebrous' side without which there would be no reflecting surface, and therefore no stopping-place for the luminous ray springing from the divine hearth. On this side of things is the mysterious will, the most direct and most intimate expression of the creature's very being. Now what does this being want if not itself? It wants itself, for it is not itself; and what it wants is its own reality, its own ontological affirmation. Such is the reason why the will wills. To want itself is to desire self-possession, to be for itself its own cause, its own origin. And so the spontaneous desire of the creature is the will for an uncreated existence. Every human being, in the primal strength of his will to be, takes himself for God, puts himself in the role of God, giving himself to himself and receiving himself from himself. This is the origin of sin since, as I have said elsewhere,[21] Adam's sin may be described as a crossing from being to an impossible self-possession. Nothing is more common than this

---

[21] *La charité profanée*, pp. 142ff.

illusion of ours, through which we want to attribute our own existence to ourselves. And how could it be otherwise? To want: is this not necessarily to want *oneself*? And would we want ourselves if we were not separated from ourselves? Can a received being ever be truly ours, we who are always a defective coincidence of essence and existence?

Enough of this! To accept oneself as creature is in reality impossible for the creature as such. What the creature desires, or even better, this desire that is creature, is, like 'ontological distance', the desire for absolute being, the desire for a divine existence. How then is it possible to consent to the 'lesser reality' of the created? There is no other possibility than the willing of the creature as creature, and it is here that the conversion of the will is effected. Who in fact wills the creature? What is the only will whose act positions the creature in being, the only 'existentiating' will, if not the uncreated Will of God? Of itself – and this is the simple truth – the creature is 'incapable' of willing. It is sometimes said: he who can do the most can do the least. But I say: *only the Most can do the least*. Only absolute Abundance can will a relative and lesser reality. It is asked: how can the multiple stem from the One; how can the relative unfold from the Absolute? And we imagine ourselves capable of grasping the relative and the multiple in themselves, an error from which derives every contradiction in philosophy. Absolute Abundance does not exclude the relative but is its sole possibility. God is the only infinite and pure Reality in whom the innumerable multitude of beings can find the 'place' to come forth and the freedom to flourish, the God whose being is not juxtaposed with or opposed to any being; the God that denies no being because he is absolute Non-position with respect to which everything has the possibility of situating itself. How would all of being be 'possible' in its ontological completeness, if not out of this 'supreme Nothing' (absolute Reality) which alone can 'give being' to everything, letting everything exist without each being contradicting all other beings? Such is the freedom of the 'children of God'.

As for its own will, the creature either wants fulness of being for itself, or else resigns itself to despair over its finiteness. Out of what 'depth' is it possible then to want oneself to be totally and absolutely, joyously and with love, such as we are in our finiteness, if not out of the same Will of God who has willed this creature that I am? To want what is, that is everything. But to want what is only makes sense through the identification of our will with the creative Will of God.

As we have just glimpsed, deification is somehow identified with creation, and this is why Meister Eckhart can declare: 'In the same being of God where God is above being and above distinction, there I myself was, there I willed myself and committed myself to create this man.'[22] Far from effacing the creature, deification alone makes it possible for it to exist in its integral truth. If deification were equivalent to a negation of the creature, it would be a sheer contradiction, since to negate the creature is to negate the creative Will of God and therefore God himself. Deification is, to the contrary, the only possible affirmation of the creature. This is what 'doing the will of God' means. 'Fiat voluntas tua sicut in cælo et in terra': Father, what you have willed in the heaven of your Word, the divine 'place' of the archetypes of all creatures, may I will it upon the earth of creation, may I will this same creation with your own uncreated Will.

The grace of the active assumption of finiteness is conferred on us by the Passion of Christ's dying on the Cross. 'Abandoned' of God, he renounces the 'God' of his natural will and goes, with a single loving rush, right to the end, right to the exhaustion of created being. In him the human will, espousing in a mortal and crucifying union the creative Will of divine Love, accepts being only what it is; it wills its own ontological finiteness, it accomplishes the infinite Will of the Father.

---

[22] Sermon 52: 'Beati pauperes spiritu'; *Meister Eckhart, the Essential Sermons*, trans. E. Colledge and B. McGinn (New York: Paulist Press, 1981), p. 202.

Appendix

The Luther Question

For about half a century the Luther question has been an object of renewed interest on the part of Catholics. An attitude of condemnation and rejection has given way to an attitude of understanding, or, at least, attentive enquiry. My intention is not to treat the question as a 'Lutherologist', which I am not by any means. Luther's written work is enormous (123 volumes in the Erlangen-Frankfurt edition, 1826–1926, noted as 'Erl.' in the references, and 67 volumes in the Weimar edition, 1883–1948, noted as '*WA*': 'Weimar Auflage'), to which must be added, since the sixteenth century, such a mass of works that an entire lifetime would not be enough to take cognisance of it all, even superficially. I would like rather to enquire briefly into the cause for this change of attitude and its significance. The hypotheses suggested here will complement what I have set forth in Chapter 1.

This change of attitude has had no effect on the declarations of the magisterium, which still maintains the incompatibility of the Catholic faith with Lutheran doctrine. But we do see it among many present-day theologians, inclined to be very disparaging of previous Roman literature on the subject. They do not so much reproach it for lack of erudition as for having constantly given itself up to criticism and polemics. In other words, the fashion of the day would have us no longer misunderstand the salutary work of the Reformer, and have us forget, or hide, the abuse and obscenities of Brother Martin, have us offer to the fine ecumenical society of our times a presentable Luther, well bred and well spoken. It is rather unlikely that he would be pleased with this.

I. This simple remark leads us to the first point of focus, to the person of the Reformation's founder, for it is in his person –

and, paradoxically, in its most disconcerting aspects – that must be found one of the major reasons for his success today. Paradoxically, yes, for Luther was not sparing in his abuse of Catholicism in general, of the Pope ('that Antichrist'), of Holy Mass, or of theology ('a work of the Devil'). Even if we make allowance for the habits of the time and for the surroundings, what remains is that Luther's coarseness, his violent invective, his rancour which goes so far as to be a tedious obsession and a quite insupportable excess of language,[1] discomfited even his contemporaries. One of his last pamphlets, clearly directed against the Pope (against the *Roman Papacy Founded by the Devil*) includes 'a scatological collection the likes of which had never been seen in a book of religious controversy'.[2]

But precisely this excess of hate seems to confer on it a pathological nature and lessen its gravity, above all at a time when one is more inclined to believe in psychoanalysis than in the Devil. Certainly, an anti-Lutheranism of the first magnitude will find itself justified by these texts. To condemn Luther not only in Catholic eyes, but in the eyes of any reasonable person, it is enough to quote him: no one has ever provided so many rods with which to have himself beaten. Let us be careful however – their very abundance makes them insignificant. Extremist and tiresome, yes, but might they not also be quite rightly the cry of a wounded soul, of a disappointed love; does not their very excess gauge the depth of the wound, the depth of his love? And there we have it: far from turning us away, after an initial revulsion they intrigue us, invite us to go further. Is he not doing the opposite of someone who is hiding what he is ashamed of? He shows it, exhibits it with a kind of desperate arrogance: yes, that's the way I am, and so much the worse for me and for you! But, beyond this filth, what accents of sincerity and piety! Once we have got over this quite justified initial revulsion, we are invited to discover a testimony of pure faith in Jesus Christ. Luther or the anti-Tartuffe. Supreme craftiness or the necessity of a crude nature? Perhaps both. In any case,

---

[1] Neither did his maledictions spare the Jews: Nazi pronouncements hardly exceed in violence the harmful words which he heaped upon them, above all in the second half of his life.

[2] J. Paquier, 'Luther', in *Dictionnaire de théologie catholique* (Paris: Letouzey et Ane, 1909–50), vol. 9, col. 1170.

the effect of a power hard to resist is there. Not only an incontestable psychopathy,[3] which is not so offensive to our contemporaries, but also a violence, a passion, a power to fascinate, which appear to be invested in a permanent and intimate relationship to Jesus Christ. It is as if this man gave us at once the lewd and revolting spectacle of his baseness, exorcising at a single stroke that baseness common to all of us, and, at the very core of this proclaimed disgrace, the upsurging of an irreducible and 'in spite of everything' faith. In this sense, and perhaps it has gone rather unmarked, Luther is eminently *modern*. From Dostoevsky to Graham Greene, passing through Anouilh and Freudism, modern culture has accustomed us to this mix of the ignoble and the sublime, which is to say basically to *this divorce of nature and grace*. For such is, I think, the most terrible error of Lutheranism. In any case, one should not doubt that sensibility does not particularly relish the spectacle of sincerity, a spectacle so much the more impressive by avowing the disparity between unworthy man and his ardour for Jesus Christ.[4]

But Luther is not only someone 'human, all too human' who, by a kind of religious psychodrama, has been delivered from his agony; he is also a rebel and conquering hero. In the name of Jesus Christ and his Gospel, this nobody, armed with his conviction, rises up – alone – against the omnipotence of Church and Pope. And, O miracle, his word is not stifled. To the contrary, and despite the combined efforts of the Roman hierarchy and the Emperor of the West, the echo of his voice resounds throughout Germany and soon Europe. Half a millennium later, there are hundreds of millions of men and women throughout the world who see themselves in him. Yes, papist Rome still stands. But how can it be denied that he has succeeded beyond all human foresight? Are there many such events in the history of mankind?

Finally, a last trait of this exceptional man, a man so like the common man by his sinful nature, by his not very lofty virtues and yet triumphant over the established powers: this man is

---

[3] I note, among others, the study by Roland Dalbiez, *L'angoisse de Luther* (Paris: Téqui, 1974).

[4] Jean-Jacques Rousseau presents an altogether analogous case.

also a religious creator, a new prophet who accomplished the most unbelievable *tour de force* – the engendering of a new Christianity. Saints and intellectual geniuses before him had practised, stressed or developed such and such an aspect of Christianity and, to some extent, enriched its development. Some heretics had isolated one truth at the expense of others, and for precisely this reason the integral body ended up rejecting them. But here we see a man rethinking the totality of religion by offering a wholly new interpretation, an interpretation that develops, grows . . . and changes the history of the world. Now what is most attractive in this matter is not so much the genius demanded for such an operation, as human character. By his example, Luther proved that religion belongs to man, that he has the right to lay his hand on this reality, sacred until then and about which the Catholic still has the feeling of knowing only one side, the other side being lost in the Invisible. With him it ceases being a mysterious object, miraculously descended from heaven and over which we have no power – everything which might admirably illustrate the immutable and hieratic power of the Roman liturgy. Luther showed everyone that he could make of it *his* thing, *his* possession, that he was the master and not the servant, that it belonged entirely to every Christian by the grace of baptism and faith, that it was for each one to be his own priest and the whole hierarchy *his alone*, and all exegesis, sacramentality and tradition as well, and that this religion was completely and only in the soul of the believer. This represents a formidable subjectivisation of our relationship with God, correlative to a general promotion to the adult state of Christians who a Mother Church held tied too long to her apron strings.

Such are, I think, the essential reasons for the seduction exercised by this astonishing figure. I would not have stressed them if it did not seem that Catholics have too often underestimated these reasons, considering some well-chosen and very incriminating quotations as proof against them.

II. But the power of the Lutheran reform is not to be reduced to the fascination exercised by one man, as agreeable as he may be to the phantasms of modern sensibility; it also consists, more durably, in the reformed Christianity that it proposes, or at the very least in what has been formed under his inspiration, for he did not follow a concerted plan, and the weight of circumstances was more determining than that of his will in the building up of this new 'religion'.[5]

Now this new Christianity, which obviously wanted a return to origins, represents by its very existence a permanent temptation for Catholics, in that it proposes a *reasonable religious solution*. A paradoxical thesis and yet true. Paradoxical if we confront it with immoderation, with the selfsame folly of a temperament filled with contradictions; but incontestable if one considers its result. We leave aside the scandals of papal Rome and the frequently denounced vices of the Church: they have played only a minor role, even though they could always be counted on to provide an easy justification for reforming projects. What characterises Catholicism, in certain respects, is that it involves the faithful in a permanent tension of the soul, in a call to holiness, in a spiritual adventure so lofty that it can at first only demonstrate our weakness and impotence: we have to merit heaven and yet 'for men this is impossible' (Mt. 19:26). Next, it plunges the faithful into a complex and hierarchical ecclesial society where they enter into relationship with differing claims and numerous people, and where one should distinguish, for example, between the hierarchy of order and the hierarchy of jurisdiction, between tradition, Scripture, the magisterium, dogmatic formulation and theological research, etc. Lastly, the Christian is invited to live in a richly diverse sacred and ritual universe, where the sevenfold Sacraments are differentiated from a host of sacramentals, where liturgical prayer and sacrificial worship are surrounded and prolonged by a swarm of devotions and practices. Adherence to this immense Body demands, for each occasion, nuance, discrimination and a faith multiplied and modulated according to the nature of its object. Lutheran religion is, to the contrary, 'reasonable' because it suppresses all notion of merit (God saves us without us); it reduces ecclesial society to the collectivity of believing individuals (the abolition of the priesthood and the power of jurisdiction); and, lastly, it denies all presence of the supernatural in the natural order (from which a multiplicity of degrees could be derived), or at

---

[5] This in particular is what the classic work by Lucien Febvre shows: *Un destin: Martin Luther* (Paris: Presses Universitaires Françaises, 1988).

least reduces it to a strict minimum: faith present in the Christian soul and Christ present in the bread and wine of the 'memorial'. What is more reasonable, more 'acceptable' than this conception? It goes straight to the 'folly of the Cross' and to mystical aspirations concentrated in a unique act of faith – would one still be Christian without that? – at the same time that it rejects everything else, and therefore wholly anticipates all of those occasions for denial by which modern rationalism has profited. Without doubt Luther was a fierce adversary of philosophy and reason: it is necessary to 'snarl' at philosophy, Thomas and Aristotle, that 'rotting [*rancidus*] philosopher'.[6] But what he reproves so violently is the use of reason in the order of faith, in theology, where one should speak only the language of Scripture; not in the natural order, where he prides himself on being as good a dialectician as anyone.

The result of this is that the Protestant religion is not so much a new Christianity as a reformed Catholicism, 'rid of everything that uselessly encumbers' and (supposedly) restored to a certain original simplicity, which means objectively a *diminished Catholicism*. If we set aside the basic problem of justification by faith, the inner spiritual principle of Lutheranism, and if we consider things from without,[7] this is incontestably the way they appear: aside from the personality of its founder, there is nothing of the bizarre or basically scandalous (for modern reason) in Protestantism, seeing that it admits belief in God, in Jesus Christ and in his Gospel.

And this is why Kant seems to be a good Lutheran when he describes 'religion within the limits of simple reason' (and not critical reason).[8] In making use of reason for theological work,

---

[6] Texts in Yves Congar, *Martin Luther: sa foi, sa réforme* (Paris: Cerf, 1983), pp. 20, 34, 36, 45, etc. The hatred of theology and philosophy is one of Luther's major obsessions, along with hatred for the Mass and above all the Pope.

[7] This point of view imposes itself for everything stemming from practical and concrete ecumenism, save for specialist colloquia, in the vast majority of cases.

[8] Of reasonable reason and not of reasoning reason. The famous declaration by which Kant summarises his whole philosophical enterprise comes to mind: 'I must therefore abolish *knowledge*, in order to find a place for *belief*' (*Critique of Pure Reason*, preface to 2nd edn.).

St Thomas subjects it to faith and supernaturalises it. By excluding reason only from the domain of faith, Luther gives it the freedom to control everything else and, in particular, everything in religion which does not stem from a purely subjective faith. This is why ecumenism is not an encounter between two sister religions, between two forms of Christianity with the same 'religious pressure' (as if we were speaking of atmospheric pressure), but between two forms of Catholicism, one with high and the other with low pressure. And meteorology tells us which way the wind blows. Thus the balance is not equal, the disequilibrium is patent, and this, whatever the good will and prudence of the mediating parties, by virtue of the very nature of things. Let us dismiss all bias and resentment, and set the terms for an ecumenical encounter of the most neutral and 'indifferent' kind. What should the Protestant religion *abandon* in order to meet with Catholicism? Nothing. On the contrary, it would be necessary for it to generate a multitude of elements, beliefs and practices. Only the one who has more *is able to* abandon this more to meet with the one who has less. They will maintain that this less is, in itself, worth more. Let us admit it – this changes nothing. Only Catholicism can become Protestant, because Protestantism is, in fact, a transformed and reduced Catholicism. How could ecumenical communication function in the reverse direction? Have we ever seen a river flow uphill?[9]

III. But I must now enquire more precisely into the nature of the inner and formative principle of Lutheranism: justification by faith. I would like simply to recall that this principle not only represents a heresy for theology, but even for philosophy.

The five-hundredth anniversary of the Reformer's birth has given rise to some odd manifestations, aimed at transforming

---

[9] It is true then that Luther did not in fact want to found 'another' religion, and that the Lutheran Church is indeed a 'provisional Church' (*Interimkirche*), a parenthesis, while awaiting the complete Lutheranisation of Catholicism, that is to say her return to her 'original truth'. One eminent Protestant, an observer at the Second Vatican Council, has thus compared the situation of Catholicism occupied by the 'Roman tyranny' to that of France in 1940, Lutheranism being identified with de Gaulle's London 'government in exile'. Cf. Congar, *Martin Luther*, p. 78.

him into a kind of Church Father. Some even consider him to be the greatest genius of Christianity, as the one who has most brilliantly 'rethought' the totality of the Christian religion according to its most authentic unifying truth. The 'revelation'[10] which Luther had about Christ constitutes, according to them, the discovery (or rediscovery) of the 'true Christian faith'. Catholics have only two things to do: ask forgiveness for the unspeakable conduct of the Church whose inheritors, alas!, they are, by ridding themselves of 'confessional shackles'; and lend an ear at last to this monk in whom the authentic Word resounds. Such methods, without effect on a competent theologian, are all-powerful over Catholics of good will, and even over numerous priests inclined to ignore the importance of doctrinal learning in the name of charity. This is why I have to specify what forms the basis of Lutheran theology, namely, justification by faith, to appreciate the soundness of its scriptural underpinnings, and to show the consequences which flow from it.

Obviously I am calling into question neither the sincerity nor the intensity of Luther's faith, nor do I underestimate the exemplary power of his convictions,[11] since it is clear, to the contrary, that they exercise a kind of imperious fascination over many Catholics: as if they were rediscovering, in the spectacle of the Reformer, what to believe about Christ. They react to his texts as if they were revelation itself: they feel themselves seized and carried away by the torrent of a living faith whose very possibility seemed to have been exhausted. By clearing away and tearing apart the tangle of rules and the undergrowth of

[10] This expression is attributed to him by Father Daniel Olivier, a professor at the Institut Catholique, in the newspaper *La Croix*, 18–19 September 1983. And we learn in the same newspaper that, according to a work by Albert Greiner, *Martin Luther: un passionné de vérité* (a work intended for young people), the Reformer, this 'knight', this 'soldier of the Gospel', was also 'a defender of the peasants'. Let us recall then what he wrote on 5 May 1525, in the midst of the Peasants' Rebellion: 'It is necessary to stop the peasants, to cut their throats, to sift them at sword's edge, in secret and public alike. Nothing is more venomous, more noxious, more diabolical than a rebel' (*WA*, vol. 18, p. 358). Harsh defender!

[11] The scandalous spectacle exhibited at times by Renaissance Rome, the spectacle of an artificial paganism which triumphed in literature, the arts and entertainment, even in the heart of the Vatican, is also in Luther's favour.

dogmatic institutions, this man rediscovered the gushing spring. What matter the excessive language or temperament, or even the doctrinal condemnations, with respect to this breakthrough to the rush of running water!

However, there is no such thing as a purely lived subjectiveness which does not involve a system of speculative principles (either philosophical or theological), the extraction of which concerns the intellect alone. This law suffers no exception, and only expresses the nature of things. Psychology implies logic, just as skin and muscle imply the skeleton: they move both themselves and other things, but according to the structure and articulations of the bony framework, however invisible. In the same way the deeply felt faith of Lutheranism, a kind of radical existentialism of our relationship to Christ, this wine which seems so strong, so intoxicating, contains and conveys a certain theological doctrine, a doctrine which can only lead to those consequences that flow from it *logically*.

Now, even though intelligible, this doctrine is false and contradictory. Once again, this does not have to do with Luther's intentions but with the objective reality of the principle of his approach. One can indeed dismiss theology and refuse to be subjected to its jurisdiction, deny its exercise. But the proof of this idea's obscurity is that, even today after five hundred years of analysis and discussion, those who study Luther continue to ask themselves about its significance. What did Luther mean? What interpretation should be given to the founding and decisive principle of the Reformation?

Essentially,[12] the Lutheran thesis has arisen from an uncontrollable agony, the agony of damnation. The monk Luther, during assuredly terrifying crises of unspeakable horror, experienced the feeling that no work, however meritorious in itself, can appease the divine justice of God: owing to omnipresent sin, neither fasts, mortifications, charitable acts, masses nor prayers have the least value. Man's nature is so thoroughly corrupt that his best actions, even the holiest, are intrinsically

---

[12] That is, leaving aside everything else (nominalism, excessive Augustinianism, his evolving thought, the pressure of events, etc.) and following what Luther himself declared in 1545, in the preface which he wrote for the edition of his Latin works, and where he relates the 'event of the tower'.

tainted, vicious, diabolical. Objectively, Luther was in the position of a man with a powerful vitality (and therefore without suicidal tendencies), but suffering from an obsessional neurosis tied to an aggressive and morbid self-hatred. To escape this obsession, he elaborated a 'mental set' which allowed him to *neutralise* his panicky fear of hell, without for all that abolishing the hateful and violent scorn for his own nature. This more or less conscious mental set abruptly crystallised (in 1518?), while reading an often considered passage from the epistle to the Romans (1:17), when its meaning suddenly began to dawn on him: 'The justice of God is revealed in the Gospel, as it is written: *the just shall live by faith.*' This justice, he suddenly understood, is not a justice-act (to render justice, to judge), but a justice-state (to be just).

Having gained this insight, here is Luther's reasoning. The justice-state (or passive justice) is that of Christ, it *is* Christ himself, in the words of St Paul. How is it to be conferred on us? By inner penetration? But then I myself would *be* just! Now this is impossible since I *am* sin. No, it is imputed to us from without: the redemption of Christ, by which we have been justified, lets us remain inveterate sinners as long as we live; it simply covers us like a mantle and saves us from damnation by granting, not that we should no longer sin, but only that our sins will no longer be imputed as crimes. This is why it is normal that works are of no use. To assert for one moment that a human work might be of value for a redemptive co-operation, the so-called sacrificial work of the Mass above all, is equivalent to denying the crucifixion: this is an abominable blasphemy, and amounts to a lack of faith in Jesus Christ alone. Such is the first point.

Now I know that the insurmountable shame of my nature is not the *proof* of my damnation, since Christ saves us 'in spite of ourselves', from without. Still, in order to heal the obsession with hell, I need to apply this certitude to myself. How do I know that I, *I myself*, am saved? What infallible *sign* attests to this? St Paul tells us: it is faith. God asks nothing of the creature, that filthy sinner, but just one thing: faith in Jesus Christ. If I have faith, I am saved. The fact of faith, within me, is the proof that Jesus Christ has indeed saved me, *I myself*. But to have faith is to believe precisely that only Jesus Christ saves me, and therefore to reject with horror all faith in works, otherwise I would not believe in Jesus Christ but in myself. Thus forensic (exterior) justification and the faith-sign of justification join and mutually condition each other. Such is the second point.

That Jesus Christ alone saves us has always been known and taught by the Church; but that St Paul clearly expounds forensic justification and the faith-sign is quite simply untenable. Luther's exegesis is false or, rather, aberrant.[13] Here I shall refer to all that I have said in *La charité profanée*. The idea that human nature, in its very own substance, remains completely outside the grace of redemption so that we are both sinners and just at the same time ('simul peccator et justus')[14] is purely Lutheran. What Luther denies is that Christ, who is in fact our Justice, the one in whom and by whom we have been restored to the state of original justice and even to a more admirable state, makes his justice 'dwell' within us, infusing it into our very being: 'The Christian is just and holy with a foreign or extrinsic holiness; he is just by the mercy and the grace of God. This mercy and this grace are not in man; they are not a *habitus* or a quality in the heart.'[15] In short, this justice is not inherent to the substance of our being, but remains on the surface, 'like a painting on a wall', Luther tells us.

Now, without speaking of St Peter, who declares us 'partakers of the divine nature', the Pauline conception of our baptismal participation in the death of Christ, the theme of the transformation of the old man into the new, the theme of the communication of the Holy Spirit, who 'unites himself with the spirit of man', for 'he who is joined to the Lord *is one spirit*' (I Cor. 6:17), all these and many other texts clearly demonstrate that Scripture is ignorant of the Lutheran thesis in its specifics.[16]

[13] Even Father Congar admits this: 'the Lutheran doctrine of justification coincides neither with Catholic doctrine nor even, as recognised by many Protestant exegetes, with the thought of St Paul' (*Martin Luther*, p. 145).
[14] WA, vol. 56, p. 272: 'Is he perfectly just then? No, but sinner and just at the same time: sinner as to the truth of the matter, just by imputation and promise.'
[15] WA, vol. 40b, p. 354.
[16] In its specifics, but not in all of its formulations, which are often orthodox. What matters here, however, is the unyielding core of the Lutheran thesis.

But, finally, we need to arrive at the philosophico-theological consequences. Basically, and whatever may have been his good intentions, this thesis rests on the radical incompatibility of nature and grace, or rather on the irreducible opposition and the mutual exclusion of the natural and the supernatural orders, which grace comes to reconcile specifically, since this grace always flows from the unique hypostasis of Christ[17] in which divinity has been united to humanity. Here, to the contrary, supernature can only work by destroying nature, and it is most difficult for us to consider such a thesis other than as 'dia-bolical', to the extent that it performs a divisive work (*dia-ballein*). Into the heart of every Christian it introduces an insurmountable separation between what stems from the creature and what stems from the redemptive act. It closes nature in upon itself, dooming it to sin, and, with the selfsame stroke, shuts up the door of heaven which Christ has opened to us. By Lutheran decree, divine grace has been forbidden to *take root* in our human earth. Henceforth our world is cleared of the sacred. Symbolism (*sym-ballein*) – in which the created and the Un-created are espoused, in imitation of Mary, Bride of the Holy Spirit, who 'reunites' (*sym-ballein*, Lk. 2:19) all things 'in her heart' – is driven from our Christian existence in the name of God's honour. No earthly form, no human work, no act is a bearer of Christ's grace – a jealous and greedy Christ who no longer *confides* the strength of his redemptive love to the weakness or to the dignity of his noble creature, nor, through the intermediary of a human consecrator, to things themselves. What disappears in this way is the 'immanence of grace' of Christ the Redeemer in his creation; that is, the sacramental and ritual order, the ecclesial order, the Mystical Body, all of this sacralising of the earthly and the human cosmos which is the Incarnation prolonged, spread abroad and communicated, as the image of the first-fruits of the 'new heaven and the new earth'.

Doubtless we will be told that a complete profanation of the natural order is correlative to an interiorisation of our relation-

---

[17] The dogma of the hypostatic union, or the union of the divine and human natures in the unique hypostasis (or person) of the Son, defined at Chalcedon in 451, caused problems for Luther: for him, human nature is a pure instrument of divine nature, without autonomy. Luther is instead a monothelite.

ship to Christ, since the only earthly sign of the divine which remains is faith, and what was lost there is gained here. However, we need to be precise. Is the Lutheran faith a supernatural reality *in* the human soul? A *habitus*? The reply is not easy, for the texts are contradictory. But no doubt is possible as to the general trend of its conception. What is emphasised here almost exclusively[18] is the human dimension of faith, faith as the human act, the human will within mercy. It is a faith *felt* by the believer, faith reduced to the subjective experience of faith and not properly a *theological* faith, in which spiritual reality is by no means perceptible to ordinary consciousness. Now, if grace remains exterior to man, do we not remain exterior to grace? Hence Luther's need to overemphasise the volitional and the sentimental dimension of the act of faith; in short, to proceed with a *psychologisation of the spiritual*.[19] This psychologisation seems characteristic of all Lutheranism, particularly its deforming of the themes of Tauler's mysticism. What is with the mystics spiritual, that is to say ontological (hence the creature's nothingness *relative* to Divine Being), with Lutheranism becomes misery, unhappiness, despair, damnation.

Finally, after the theological and spiritual consequences, we turn to the philosophical consequences. The mutual exclusion of the natural and supernatural orders is not only ruinous for the sacredness of the cosmos and spiritual interiority, it is equally destructive in the long run of human reality as such; for the ontological consistency of the human is established and assured only by its ordination to the divine. We must ever return to the witness of Genesis: the nature of the human being is its deiformity. Deiform by essence, we should fulfil our ontological destiny as image of God and *become likeness*, for, as St Paul informs us, 'we are of the race of God' (Acts 17:29). Without doubt human nature cannot by itself – not even with Adam – realise its supernatural perfection. But it is solely this possible relationship to a future realisation which defines and guarantees our present reality. This is why there is no purely naturalist humanism. Reduced to itself, human nature is in no way a

---

[18] And necessarily, given its value as sign, as an inner criterion for salvation.
[19] On the distinction between the psychic and the spiritual, cf. *La charité profanée* (Bouère: Editions Dominique Morin, 1979), part I and *passim*.

starting-point. If man does not turn to God, he will seek his final cause and the principle for his illusory completion in the world and in matter.

Profanation of the world, psychologisation of the Spirit, secularisation of the human being, such are the three ineluctable consequences inscribed in the founding principle of Lutheranism. The residual strength of a deeply Christian sensibility prevented Luther from perceiving them, and their development within Protestantism would be stifled directly by virtue of the Gospel and indirectly by the stimulating example of an intact Catholicism. But, with the efforts of the Catholic neo-Lutherans, are not these last safeguards today in the process of collapsing?

Central to the drama of Luther is an insurmountable aversion with respect to his own human nature, which was created by God in his image, but consigned by Luther to total corruption. Without doubt, this aversion was only the other side of that fascination which his own individuality exercised on him, even in its coarsest aspects: the secret of a powerful and tormented man, capable of tenderness for a flower, a bird, a child, but who never succeeded in humbly taking pity on himself and looking into his own poor heart with the mercy of God. Here, with the exclusion of a nature entirely fallen from grace, the sense of the supernatural is no longer nurtured, and yet this same nature is aggressively reclaimed in the pride of its finiteness.

Index of Names and Subjects

Abel, 86
Adam, xiii, 15, 80–1, 90–2, 101
adoption, 115, 117–9, 133
Æterni Patris, 29
Alger, 107
Alphonsus de Liguori, St, 129
Amalaire of Metz, 71
Ambrose, St, 69
angelism, 32
Aquinas, St Thomas, 18, 24, 29, 100, 115, 117–18, 135, 148, 149
  Summa Contra Gentiles, ix
  Summa Theologiae, ix–x, 13–14, 34, 69, 83, 95, 122, 133, 136
Aristotle, xi, 100, 146
Arius, 8
Augustine of Hippo, St, 105, 127

Babel, 101
Barth, Karl, 99
Bartmann, Mgr, 106
Basil the Great, St, 134
Bernanos, 55, 56
Bernard of Clairvaux, St, 125
Blondel, Maurice, xii
Blood of Christ, 17, 84–9, 92, 106, 119
Body of Christ, 69–79, 85–9, 93–9, 110, 119
Borella, Jean
  Charité profanée, 102, 111, 131, 138, 153
  Ésotérisme guénonien et mystère chrétien, 116
Bossuet, 51

Cajetan, 29

Cartesianism, 50
Catechism of the Catholic Church, 42
Christianity, ideological, 1, 6, 21
circumincession, 84
Clement of Alexandria, 18
Congar, Yves, 148, 149, 153
contact, entitative, 127, 128, 136
Corpus Christi, see Body of Christ
Cyril of Alexandria, St, 116, 120

Dalbiez, Roland, 145
deification, 115, 130, 132, 134, 137, 140
Descartes, René, 50
Dionysius the Areopagite, 115–16
divinisation, 82, 83, 85
Drewermann, Eugen, 3, 39

Eckhart, Meister, 115, 124, 137, 140
ecumenism, 12

faith, 2, 8, 10, 16, 19, 20, 26–7, 150
  justification by, 9, 150
Febvre, Lucien, 147
fideism, Protestant, 18
filiation, 82, 88, 115
freedom, divine, xi

Galileo, 25
Gamber, Mgr Klaus, 63
Gilson, Etienne, 30
gnosis, 18
Godescalc, 71
Gonet, 83
grace, x, xi, 14, 80–2, 108–10, 145, 154

157

Gregory Naziantus, St, 134
Gregory of Nyssa, St, 83, 133
Greiner, Albert, 150
Guénon, René, 92, 123

habitus, 108, 153, 155
　entitative, 14, 15, 18, 40
　operative, 14
heart, 26, 57, 87, 91, 95, 108, 130, 135-6
　eye of the, 17, 20, 40
heresy, 3, 6-9, 12, 19-20, 28
hermeneutics, 3, 109
　Christian, 107
　modern, 27
Hilary of Poitiers, St, 119-20
Hippolytus, St, 48
Honorius of Autun, 72
Humani Generis, x

image of God, 15, 34, 71, 80, 155
intellect, 8, 13, 15, 138, 151
Irenaeus, St, 18, 129

Jerome, St, 105
Jesus, Name of, 108-9
John Chrysostom, St, 105
John of the Cross, St, 127-30, 135-6
John Paul II, Pope, 43
Justin, St, 107

Kant, Immanuel, 148
kenosis, 82, 85, 87
Küng, Hans, 3, 39

Laneau, Mgr Louis, 115-26
Lefèbvre, Mgr, 42
Leibniz, 52
Leo XIII, Pope, 29
Loisy, Alfred, 20, 37, 39
Lombard, Peter, 105
Lubac, Henri de, ix, xiii, 30, 71, 106
Luther, Martin, 8-11, 31-2, 143-56

Maritain, Jacques, 127
Marxism, 17

Mary, the Blessed Virgin, 3-4, 26, 71, 81-2, 92, 96, 108-9, 112, 134
　coronation of, 135
Mary Magdalene, St, 94
Mass, 4, 31, 61, 63-4
metanoia, 76, 82, 87
modernism, x, xiii, 17, 20, 23, 27-8, 30, 34-6, 40, 43
Montesquieu, 64
Maximus the Confessor, St, 8, 135

name, divine, 108
naturalism, xi
nature, ix-xii, 80, 134, 145, 154
　human, 82
neo-Thomism, 30, 127
Nestorius, 8
Nietzsche, 33
Novus Ordo, 47, 63, 65

Oath, anti-Modernist, 28
Olivier, Father Daniel, 150
Origen, 97, 109

paradise, 10, 26, 90-2
Paquier, J., 142
Pascendi, 20
Paschasius Radbertus, St, 71, 74
Paul VI, Pope, 63
philosophy, x, xiii
　Scholastic, xii
　of nature, 53
Pius X, Pope St, 20
Pius XII, Pope, 47
plērōma, 83, 89
potency, obediential, 134

rationalism, Kantian, x
Ratzinger, Joseph Cardinal, 43
reason, xii-xiii
revelation, xi
Rousseau, Jean-Jacques, 145

Sabellius, 8
Satan, 91
schism, Greek, 12
science, x, xii, 5, 24
Scripture, 97-112

Index of Names and Subjects

sense of the supernatural, xi–xiii,
   15–19, 23, 26, 30, 32, 34,
   37–40, 43, 59, 61, 65, 99,
   115, 127, 156
Seraphim of Sarov, St, 121
Sertillanges, Father, 136
sin, original, 80–1, 92–4
Suarez, 134
supernaturalism, xi–xii, 134
supernature, ix–x, 134
symbolism, 54, 154
synthesis
   paradigmatic, 83–5
   prototypical, xi
   sacramental (and redemptive),
     84–5

Teresa of Avila, St, 129–30, 135

Theresa of the Child Jesus, St, 18
theology, 4, 9, 24
   of culture, 30
theomorphism, 90
Thomas (the Apostle), St, 94
Thomism, 30
tradition, 33, 54–6, 99
Trent, Council of, 8, 14
Trinity, 70, 84, 119, 122

Vatican II, x, 20, 28–9, 42
Vatican Council, First, 2, 28

will, 9, 15, 13, 81–2, 109, 137–40
William of Saint-Thierry, 106
wisdom, divine, xi
Word, the, 4, 79, 82, 93, 96–9, 109,
   117, 119, 129

Index of Scripture References

Old Testament

Exod.
- 33:23 — 128

Ps.
- 35:10 — 131
- 50:10 — 34
- 82:6 — 129

Song of Sol.
- 2:17 — 126

Ecclus.
- 17:8 — ii

New Testament

Matt.
- 5:8 — 17
- 7:21 — 108

Luke
- 2:19 — 154
- 5:32 — 82
- 10:22 — 131
- 17:37 — 71
- 18:8 — 26
- 18:19 — 90

John
- 3:13 — 60
- 6:57 — 119
- 10:34 — 133
- 17:21 — 119
- 20:17 — 94

Acts
- 10:40–1 — 95
- 17:27–28 — 133
- 17:28 — 40

Rom.
- 1:17 — 152
- 5:14 — 107
- 6:3–5 — 88
- 8:22 — xi
- 8:29–30 — 132
- 10:10 — 17

1 Cor.
- 6:17 — 153
- 13:12 — 132

2 Cor.
- 1:22 — 17
- 3:18 — 125
- 5:17 — 89
- 5:21 — 93

Eph.
- 1:4 — 76
- 1:15–8 — 17
- 2:10 — 76

Phil.
- 2:5–7 — 82

Col.
- 1:15 — 125
- 1:15–6 — 76
- 2:6 — 123
- 3:3 — 125
- 3:9 — 17

Heb.
- 1:3 — 125
- 6:4 — 17
- 9:24 — 95, 107
- 11:1 — 19

1 Pet.
- 1:19–20 — 89
- 3:21 — 107

2 Pet.
- 1:3–4 — 129
- 1:4 — 88, 116

1 John
- 3:1 — 116, 129

Apoc.
- 21:1 — 89